In celebration of

KINGSTON SEYMOUR
All Saints Church of England
Voluntary Controlled
Primary School

KINGSTON SEYMOUR SCHOOL

Somerset

The Root of Village Life
1858 – 1968

By

Marion Pudner
&
Sue Thomas

The cover illustration is reproduced from the original architect's drawing. Noticeably, the central roof window was eventually built differently from this original design.

First published in Great Britain 2008 by
J.R. Marketing
41 High St. Chipping Sodbury
Bristol BS37 6BA

A CIP catalogue record for this book
is available from the British Library

ISBN 978-0-9540430-2-5

Contents

Dedication

This book is dedicated to the memory of Joan Ridley, whose love for her village created the basis of this text. The following dedication had already been prepared by her, just a short time before she died.

Kingston Seymour village school closed in 1968. I, together with my brothers and sister, had been pupils there - as had my father and his sister before us. During the 1990s, I became curious as to when the school opened and so began my research at the Taunton Record Office.

The school plans revealed it had opened during 1858. The school log books were fascinating to read, giving not only insights into the school but also some aspects of village life as it was at that time.

In 1998, with other ex-pupils still living in the village, it was arranged to have a school reunion. I continued to transcribe interesting bits from the school log books and asked around for photographs of the school and its pupils over more recent years. The earliest photograph found was dated 1871. All this was used in a display at the reunion and it was from this that I was asked to produce a book.

A few years had passed when Marion Pudner (nee Kingcott) offered her help to complete the research, collation and publishing of this book. I am very grateful to Marion and her husband Rob in achieving this.

We hope you will enjoy the book as much as we have enjoyed producing it.

Joan Ridley.

Acknowledgements

We would like to thank the many people who have helped prepare in the production of this book, which we believe to be the first full-length study published on the history of Kingston Seymour.

Thanks are due to the staff at the Somerset Record Office; David Bromwich of the Somerset Studies Library, Taunton; and also to Jane Bell and Janet Burdge of the Kingston Seymour History Society. The Record Office has been kind in allowing us to quote from the school logs and manager's minutes (A/A2P,C/E/4/290, D/P/K.sey/18/7/1).

The book would not have been possible without the contributions of memories and old photographs from ex-pupils and others (who are acknowledged in the text). Bob Ford has been particularly helpful in allowing us to use his knowledge and writings. Other people have been disturbed by late night telephone calls and had to scurry off to put pen to paper or find memorabilia. It was especially pleasing to be loaned the original watercolour sketch by Patrick Collins of the large schoolroom in use as a weaving school.

Many thanks to Rob for textual assistance and to Josh Pudner for designing the cover and scanning the photographs. Louise Pudner has helped with proof reading & technical advice.

Last of all, many thanks are due to Jim Ruston for his encouragement and help in getting the book published.

Contact details for further information or extra copies of the book: telephone Marion Pudner 01278 785627 or email robpudner@hotmail.com or suethomas.ks@hotmail.co.uk

Chapter 1
Early Days

Very little is known about education in Kingston Seymour before the building of the school. In the Church Vestry Minutes of 1792 there is mention of a general meeting of the parishioners. This resulted in another general meeting held on 3rd Dec 1792, which confirmed that a Sunday School would be started, the expense of which would be raised by an annual subscription. It was also moved that John Earl be appointed master of this weekly school, to be paid for out of the poor rates. Among the signatories are E C Grevile - Curate, John Sheppard – Church Warden, William Westoversoon, George Witherall, James Wallis, Thomas Eddington, James Bishop, Wm. Hammans and John Durbin.

In 1817 the Sunday School was still continuing as Rachel Denmead was appointed as mistress for that year 'on the same terms as usual'. By 1826 there was discussion concerning 'the expense of raising and attiring the Church Stable for the purpose of a habitation for a person helping the Sunday School.' In 1841 there also appears to have been a small boarding school in the village.

On the 23rd April 1857 an application was made for aid towards the building of schoolrooms to accommodate 60 pupils in Kingston Seymour. This was made to the National Society Promoting the Education of the Poor in the Principles of the Established Church. The application form was filled in by George Octavius Smyth-Pigott, Rector, the fourth son of Sir John Hugh Wadham Pigott Smyth Pigott of Brockley Hall. Incidentally, why this gentleman's father had two Pigotts in his name is not clear!

The Rector stated 'that as there are no resident gentry in the parish, the land-owners most of them living at a distance, that the support of the school, notwithstanding the liberality of some, will fall heavily on the clergyman of the parish, that at present the education of the children is most imperfect, owing to there being such an indifferent master, and there being no suitable accommodation for the master or the children, the parishioners anxious to obtain better provision for the education of the poor in the parish, have no other means of getting sufficient funds for the purpose of building unless they appeal to the different societies.'

The population of the parish at the time was held to be 373 people. The current provision was described as being 'next to nothing. There is a small unhealthy room in which a few children are taught reading and writing by a very old man who is utterly unfit for the office. An entire change in this provision will be made when the new schoolhouse is built. The Plymouth Brethren send a person every Sunday from Clevedon to keep a Sunday School, and this is kept up by that sect.'

Note: Kingston Chapel had not yet been built at this time. It is believed that the Brethren met in the old Quaker Meeting House, now Ashley Acre, at the top of Bullocks Lane. The Chapel in Lampley Road was built in the early 1860s. Over the years it became a Free Church Evangelical Chapel (moving away from its Brethren beginnings). The Chapel finally closed for worship in 2004.

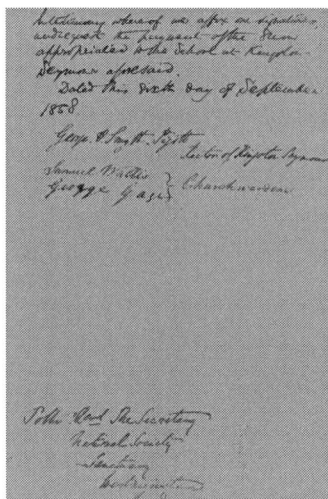

The proposed dimensions of the Schoolroom were to be 37ft by 16ft with a height of 11ft to the wall plate and 15ft to the beam. A residence for the teacher was also planned consisting of a parlour, kitchen and scullery together with three bedrooms. The form was approved and signed by Bishop Auckland (Bath and Wells).

Payment per pupil for instruction was to be a penny a week and upwards. 'The Rector of the Parish, the Lord of the Manor, and several of the Landed Proprietors would subscribe annually to the support of the school.'

The signatures on the original application.

The site was given by the Lord of the Manor, Sir John Hugh Wadham Pigott Smyth-Pigott, and the trustees to whom the site was conveyed were the Rector and the Church Wardens. Estimates of the cost were £700 although the final cost came in at £740 in total. £480 was raised by subscription and collection in the locality with the rest coming from the Society and The Committee of Council on Education.

The conveyance was dated 22nd July 1857 gifting part of an orchard rented by Charles Gould and measuring two roods (approximately half an acre). The management of the school was to be overseen by a committee consisting of the rector, his curate and six other gentlemen consisting of William Miles M.P. of Leigh

Court near Bristol, together with Samuel Wallis, Charles Gould, John Blew, John Wallis, and George Gage, all yeomen of Kingston Seymour. They were to subscribe at least twenty shillings a year towards the running of the school. The teachers and the committee members were all to belong to the Church of England. Four ladies were to assist them in the 'visitation and management of the Girls and Infant Schools'.

The first plan of the School and School House is dated 5th August 1857 and signed by John King who appears to have been the contractor while Foster and Wood, Bristol architects, did the original design drawings dated March 30th 1857.

The official opening of the school was arranged for Tuesday 27th July 1858 with Lord Auckland, Bishop of the Diocese, preaching the sermon in the morning while the Rev. Woodforde, Vicar of Kempsford, Gloucestershire, was to preach in the evening. A tea was also provided at 5 o'clock, all proceeds going on behalf of the School Building Fund.

From 1860 to 1871 the first teacher was Mr James Flack. According to the 1861 census, he had a wife and children and came from Richmond, Surrey, his wife being from Bedfordshire. There appears to be no record of a previous teacher. There may have been use of voluntary teachers during the period 1858-60. Unfortunately, there seems to be no school records for this period.

Earliest photo dated 22nd September 1871, Agnes Neades won 2nd prize for Catechism. Agnes was the mother of Kay Baker and Win Bunstone (nee Webber)

Chapter 2
Mr Turner and the First Log Book

From 1872 to 1875 the teacher was Mr A Turner.

The earliest School Log Book found was first started in 1873 following the introduction of the new national regulations in 1872. These regulations are printed inside the front cover of the first Kingston Seamour (sic) Log book, part of which reads as follows:

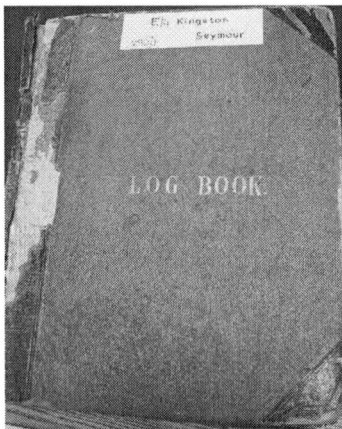

'The Principal teacher must make at least once a week in the Log Book an entry which will specify ordinary progress and other facts concerning the school or its Teachers – such dates of withdrawals, commencement of duty, cautions, illness which may require to be referred to at a future time, or may otherwise deserve to be recorded... No reflections or opinions of a general character are to be entered in the log book.'

The Kingston Seymour Log Book commences as follows with its original spellings and punctuation. The entries are quoted verbatim, while extracts have been made at times to avoid repetition. If there is an unusual spelling of a word it will be indicated by 'sic'.

All Saints School Kingston Seymour. 6th Jan'y 1873

Julia Stuckey admitted to School, remained one week, then peacefully departed to roam the fields and lanes again.
James Hale visits the Master and makes use of a host of words not commonly found in the dictionary. As the above individual threatened to take the Schoolmaster's life and do several little minor "deeds of love" the Managers thought James Hale had better apologise or take his children away. James chose the latter alternative.

Jan 6th 1873 Recommenced the school after the Xmas Holidays. Attendance small in consequence of the miserable state of the weather.

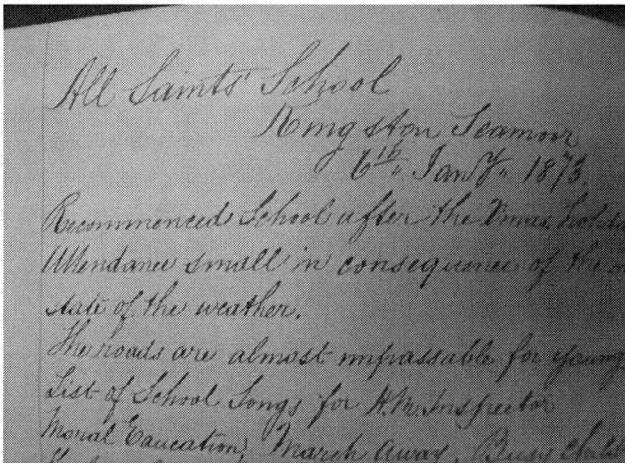

The first entry in the earliest surviving log book with an early spelling of the village name

Jan 7th 1873 The roads are almost impassible for young children. List of school songs for H M Inspector Moral Education, March Away, Busy Children, The Cat, Lullaby, Good Order, Home! I won't be a dunce, Another Oe'r, The Snow, The Daisy and What can the Matter be?

Jan 13th 1873 The Revd. G O Smyth-Piggott hired a magic lantern and the children and their parents appeared much delighted with the views.

Jan 14th 1873 Henry Gooding of this parish summoned by the Schoolmaster for using profane language. The magistrates find a suitable place of repose for Henry, fined him 9 shillings and bind him over to keep the peace for six months.

Feb 1873 Very small attendance, heavy fall of snow, rain etc. Fair progress. Nothing of importance to record, in fact finding matter to fill this book is like having to keep a family of 10 on 9 shs a week.

Mar 3rd 1873 Mrs Palmer at Birmingham, no sewing in consequence.

Mar 10th 1873 The Rev. G. O. SP examines the children in Old Test history on Wednesday after 4 p.m. Progress fair.

Mar 17th 1873 The children examined by the Rector three afternoons this week.

Mar 24th 1873 Notice of the intended visit of the Rev.W.B. de Molegns, Diocesan Inspector of the district. Great improvement in the weather which tend to draw the children from the school to the fields to assist in setting the potatoes.

A postcard of the school dated 1901, little changed from when it was built.

Report 28th March 1873
This school is in a transition state, and from being a bad school is in course of improvement under an earnest and painstaking master. I have no doubt that next year the Inspector will have to record a marked progress. W.B. de Molegns.

May 4th 1873 School closed on Tuesday, Tythe Audit and Feast. The school resembles a huge spittoon and the smell of tobacco is too strong to be agreeable.

May 11th 1873 James Stuckey, Mark Heal, Charles Hale and Frank Bailey withdrawn from school to go to work. Emily Nash and Mary Jane Hale leave school for the summer!

June 30th 1873 School examined by H.M. Inspector R.J. Boyles. *"The work of this school is sufficiently good for a first examination. Writing poor, spelling fair and reading the best part of the work. Grant 15/5 ½ per child on the average.*

Feb 23rd 1874 Harriet Gooding leaves school for service. She is almost destitute of even the elements of plain education.

Marc9th 1874 Walter Jones expelled for bad conduct.

Apr 20th 1874 Tithe Audit and Feast. Walter Jones re-admitted.

May 12th 1874 New Code Reader, adopted into the school (Collins).

June 15th 1874 Weather hot, children languid and indisposed to work. No rain for several weeks and the ground is parched and barren. In consequence of the very scanty crop of hay, few children are required in the fields and are now getting the benefit of a little extra schooling.

June 17 1874 The monotony of a Master's life is slightly disturbed by Mrs Robert Jones who made an evening call and fully vented her spleen. When she left I felt sorry for her husband.

June 23rd 1874 St John's Day. Register marked at 8.50 and children go to the Church at 11 o'clock.

June 26th 1874 Midsummer Holidays. School closed for 3 weeks.

July 13th 1874 The Revd, G.O. Smyth-Piggott gives a treat to the school children and their parents. A large party assemble at the Sea Wall, partaking of tea and join in the sports. Prizes given by Mrs G.H. Smyth-Piggott and others.

July 22nd 1874 Notice received from the Dept. that a Grant has been awarded. Grant £35.12.0d. Government Report, London. 20th July 1874.
"This school is under good influence, carefully taught and making satisfactory improvement."

Aug 12th 1874 Half Holiday. Yatton Harvest Home. Large attendance at the Festival but the weather most miserable. Miss Hoskin goes to Yatton with some of the children.

Aug 19th 1874 Average progress, The old story i.e. Nothing to record.

Sep 15th 1874   If we subtract from the school year the times children spent in 'Apple picking',' 'Potato setting', 'Gathering', 'Haymaking', and 'Bird Minding', we come to the painful conclusion that children in agricultural districts have few opportunities of mental improvement. Time will show changes I trust.
The body of a sailor found this week on the beach.

Sep 21st 1874 The attendance canes in use in this school do not appear to have increased the attendance of those children for whose benefit they were designed. A large proportion of people in the country are quite unconcerned about the education of their children and do not care a snuff about the children and its advantages.

Oct 5th 1974   Theodore Fisher leaves the school and goes into the fields where he has an opportunity to forget his letters and to study natural philosophy.

Oct 28th 1874   Lecture on South Africa by Mr Hall. The Rector pays for all the children.

14th Dec 1874 Examination for Christmas Prizes. The Rector, Mrs Piggott and Miss Halford examines (especially Miss H). Poor Annie Bishop.

Dec 18th 1874   Christmas Holidays. School closed for two weeks.

Dec 21st 1874 The Rector gives a Christmas Treat to the children and friends. Christmas Tree Prizes. Terrific consumption of cakes etc.

1875

Jan 11th 1875 Rose Seamore admitted. She and her sister entirely innocent of a knowledge of the alphabet. The eldest about 11 (they all vanished the next day).

Jan 25th 1875 Half Holiday. Hannah Wallis leaves school for home duties. She is a farmer's daughter and has passed in the 2nd Standard only! Never mind she can write a parish note!
Note: The school examinations were arranged in a series of 'Standards' and a child was expected to move up a Standard each year.

Jan 28th 1875 School closed at 12 noon in honour of Miss Beatrice Pigott's birthday. Quite a change in the weather, but May still suffering from the late severe frost. Evening classes held in the school room by the Rev G.O. SP to prepare confirmation candidates.

Mrs Pigott visits the Seamores at Phipps Bridge and the Rector tries to induce Mr Seamore (Senr) to educate his children and places them on the Free List but they do not attend. The Venerable parent does not object to being clothed and fed but he does object to having his children taught.

Feb 20th 1875 The Agricultural Children's Act keeps a boy at school. Its weak point is the want of an officer to enforce its provision. Fancy summoning a Kingston farmer for an offence against the Act and then applying to him for his subscription in support of the school!!

Note: This Act of 1873 raised the age at which children might be employed in gangs from eight to ten years. Children below the age of eight could only work for their parents and on their parent's land..

Apr 5th 1875 A Dame School kept by 'Mother Williams'. She does not trouble about examinations and inspectors. On that day two children left the church school to attend her school.

Apr 6th 1875 There was a marked absence among the children because of heavy rain and much sickness in the whole village. There were only 21 children present and the roads are flooded.

Apr 8th 1875 Diocesan Inspector's Report on the Master's certificate.
Great credit is due to Mr Turner the Schoolmaster for having brought this school single handed to such a state of proficiency. I find a marked improvement in every department of religious knowledge. W.B. Molegns.

May 17th 1875 Whit-Monday. School closed. Children at the 'Sports' in the Rector's grounds.

June 1st 1875 Commencement of school year. Average progress.

June 8th 1875 Usual progress, weather wet and cold and the attendance scanty in consequence.

June 14th 1875 Rev. G.O. SmP. visits school, two or three children ill and some absent in open violation of the Agricultural Children's Act.

June 22nd 1875 Children and their parents had their annual treat in the Rectory grounds. A number of persons sat down to an excellent tea and most pleasant afternoon was spent by all. Mrs G.H. Piggott got up a number of races and prizes were given to the successful ones. Polly Fry won a rosette as Champion of the Girls and Frank Bailey obtained a similar honour as chief of the boys. The consumption of cakes, strawberries, tea, etc. was simply awful and many children who have not grasped simple addition managed to grasp cakes *ad infinitum.*

June 23rd 1875 Very scanty attendance, the cake vanishers are conspicuous by their absence. Yesterday about 70 or more pleaded guilty to a partiality to cake. To-day a number gape over the 6 times tables.

June 24th 1875 St John the Baptist. Register marked at 9 o'clock & the children attend church at 11 o'clock. Beautiful weather and as a natural or rather unnatural consequence the Hay monster claims its annual victims and hurries them to their doom.

July 3rd 1875 Miserable attendance.

July 12th 1875 School closes for Midsummer Holidays.

July 21st 1875   Govt. Inspector's Report. "This School has considerably improved since I examined it two years ago. The order is good."

July 23rd 1875 Handed over school materials to Managers.

July 24th 1875   In leaving this school we beg to express out thanks to the Rev. G.O. Smyth-Piggott, Rector, and Mrs Smyth-Piggott and all the members of the family for their great kindness to us during the past three years. Few days have passed in which we have not been indebted to their kindness in some way or other. To Mrs Piggott my thanks is especially due, not only, for her kindness and warm hearted sympathy to me and mine, but also for the great interest she has taken in the success of the school, and for her weekly lessons, examinations etc. scripture, music and other subjects. We have always found both Mr and Mrs Piggott ready on all occasions to promote the happiness of the teachers and the welfare of the children. Our chief regret in leaving is that we have so much kindness and can give so poor a return.
A Turner.

Chapter 3
Mrs Blanche Jackson 1875-82

Oct 25th 1875 Reopened school after it having been closed for 3 months. The children are, in consequence, most unruly.

Nov 3rd 1875 Used the cane on E. Gooding.

Nov 8th 1875 Began the week with determination that the children should not eat apples during school hours, a fault they are greatly addicted to.

Nov 12th 1875 Mrs Piggott sent 6 coconuts to be divided amongst the children, at least those who deserve it.

Nov 15th 1875 It was decided to leave the school room open for the children during dinner hour, which is, I think, a bad plan.

Nov 17th 1875 The children are unusually troublesome.

Nov 21st 1875   Obliged to have half-holiday on account of the smoke.

Dec 9th 1875 We had a holiday in order to have the schoolroom chimney cleaned.

Dec 13th 1875 We had a visit from a clergyman, name unknown, he gave the children a few words of good advice.

Dec 20th 1875   We had a visit from Mr Turner the late Schoolmaster, the children seemed pleased to see him, with the exception of Edwin Gooding, who no doubt remembered his frequent, but deserved punishments.

1876

Jan 11th 1876   Reopened School after Christmas Holidays, the children quiet and attentive with the exception of the two Goodings, who are a trial to anyone's patience.
We had a visit from a clergyman, who has some idea of examining here.

Jan 19th 1876 Mrs Jackson took the boys to their writing and spoke about the dirt made in the school room during dinner hour.

Feb 28th 1876 The women's club was today taken in the school.

Feb 29th 1876 Mr Barnwell gave a scripture lesson in the school today.

Mar 15th 1876 We let the children out of school at half past eleven to see the Wedding Party leave the Church.

Mar 17th 1875 Mr Barnwell did not give his usual scripture lesson today.

Mar 20th 1876 A man came today to see to the broken window, he said he had not proper tools with him, and would come again on Wednesday.

Mar 22nd 1876 The children are much improved in their behaviour, and are consequently progressing with their lessons.

Mar 27th 1876 The windows are still unmended. There is nothing to state about the School.

Mar 30th 1876 We closed School at 12 o'clock to-day, the man came to see to the window, but after all, only to take the measurement.

Apr 3rd 1876 A very large School, the children orderly and attentive.

Apr 11th 1876 We have a small School to-day owing to the wet, the windows are still unmended.

Apr 26th 1876 Closed School to-day for the Tithe Audit. Revd. G.O. Smyth-Pigott, & family return home, it is delightful to have them back again.

May 1st 1876 We have a large School to-day. Henry & Arthur Denmead farmer's sons come for the first time.

May 2nd Mrs Pigott & Miss Ethel take classes in school today which is a great help!!!

May 3rd 1876 The following is a copy of a Report sent by the Diocesan Inspector of Schools.
' The closing of the School for 4 months of last Autumn & other adverse circumstances have thrown the school back sadly. The

present Teacher seems to have done her duty conscientiously &
with some provision during her three months of office.

Pictures are wanted for the little ones, and
an efficient Monitor, at least, with some
assistance from the clergy, if the lower
portion of the school is to do well.'

A writing slate discovered by
Roland Griffin in the ditch
behind the school.

May 16th 1876 The children are working
well trying to prepare for their
examinations.

May 22nd 1876 The children began their paper work to-day. Mrs
Pigott kindly taken them to their Dictation.

May 25th 1876 Ascension Day. Children attended Church at 11
o'clock, afterwards assembled at the Rectory, where they received
a bun each. School closed for the afternoon.

May 31st 1876 Mrs Pigott took a class for reading and also looked
at their writing.

June 12th 1876 We have received notice of the Inspector's visit to
this School, it is fixed for the 28th of this month.
List of School Songs for H.M. Inspector,
The old ones are: Old England Forever; Smiling May; Waking
Bird; March Away; Merrily March Always; I won't be a Dunce.
The new ones: Goodbye to Summer; The Lark; Music Everywhere;
Speak Gently; Beautiful Star; The Prairie Flower.
For the Infants: A Neat Little Clock; Little Bird; Twinkle Twinkle
Little Star; The Puss; Hop,Hop,Hop; The Lark.

Oct 16th 1876 We closed school to-day for the Tithe Audit, and
shall not open again until Monday next as the room must be well
cleaned before it will be fit for use.

Oct 25th 1876 The 3rd Standard began their samplers to-day.

Dec 8th 1876 We closed school to-day for a week in order that I
might attend the Gov. examinations at Salisbury.

1877

Feb 28th 1877   Closed school to-day in order to have the room prepared for a supper in honour of the coming-of-age of Mrs Pigott's eldest son. We shall not re-open until Monday as the room must be washed.

Note: this meant the school closing for the Thursday and Friday.

Oct 25th 1877   I have had charge of this school two years to-day. I trust I may have done a little good for the children.

Nov 1st 1877   All Saints'. Took the children to church. They behaved shamefully for which I have given them a severe punishment.

Nov 5th 1877   Commenced the club for the year. This club has in most cases had a good effect upon the children's attendance.

1878

Sep 3rd 1878   Bags given to the children to carry their Home Lessons in.

Sep 11th 1878   We have a small school to-day owing to the rustic Sports which are carried on in the Rectory field. I find it better to close the school for the afternoon.

1879

Feb 20th 1879   Infants finished their first patchwork quilt.

Sep 6th 1879   Fresh patchwork for the Infants.

Nov 1st 1879   Moved children's desks nearer the fire.

Nov 10th 1879   Closed the school to-day, the room being required for a meeting of the rate-payers to consider how the school is to be supported.

Nov 12th 1879   It was agreed at the meeting on Wednesday to continue to support the school by voluntary subscriptions.

Nov 18th 1879   The committee have given me 10 shs to buy the sewing required by the girls.

1880

Jan 19th 1880   Obliged to close the school. The snow being so deep it is impossible for the children to come.

Oct 14th 1880   Very small school owing to rough wind. It is really unsafe for them to be out. Several tiles blown off.

1881

Oct 25th 1881   Had charge of school 6 years to-day.

Oct 28th 1881   The young Squire Mr C. Piggott of age to-day. During dinner hour every child had a bun and a 3d piece given to them, Mr S Griffin distributed them. The Bells rang all day.

1882

Apr 18th 1882   Mrs B. Williams called, not very civil. Thought her boys were working too hard.

Apr 21st 1882   Sent in my resignation to-day in the committee meeting.

Apr 27th 1882   A committee meeting at which they decide to try to get a Master.

May 9th 1882   Mrs Coombs fined a shilling for child's bad attendance.

May 31st 1882   School year ends to-day.

July 14th 1882   Closed school to-day.

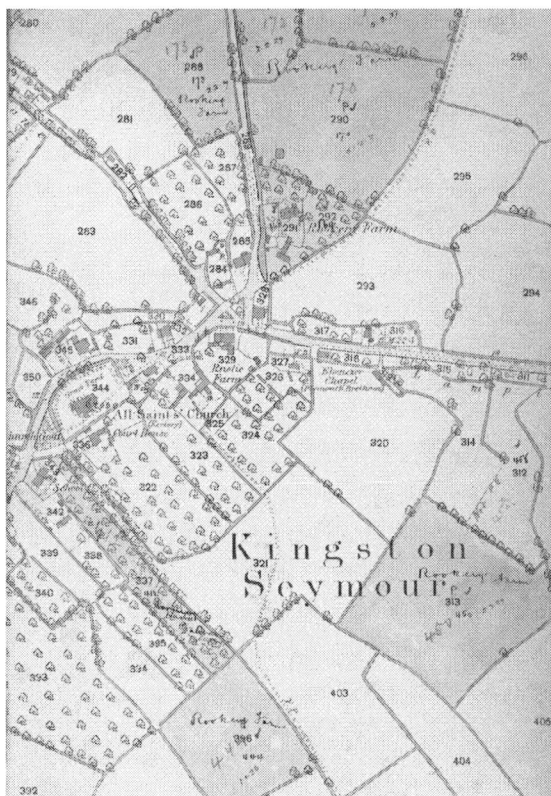

An OS map of 1886 of the village centre shows the school on the middle left hand edge. There are a large number of orchards all around the school.

Chapter 4
The Smiths & The Smyth-Pigotts

Mr James Smith was born March 17th 1855 and was a pupil at St Paul's National Boys School, Bristol. He was reputed to have walked to Yatton Station from Kingston every day to collect a London newspaper.

Aug 7th 1882   James Smith holding certificate of 3rd class has commenced duties as Master of this school. Number of children in the morning 14. I suppose this number is owing to 4 weeks holiday having been given in previous years. The scholars say they were not informed by Miss Jackson how long the holidays were to last. I find that looking at the registers that although Miss Jackson was here for 7 weeks after the school year began she has entered no school fees nor has she filled up the register during that time.

Aug 9th 1882 Mrs Piggott sent a piece of oil-cloth for the Master's desk.

Aug 14th 1882 Mrs Smith will take the Infants.

Aug 28th 1882 Mrs Smith took the sewing again this afternoon. Taught them to cut out patterns.

Oct 24th 1882   Owing to very heavy rains the roads are much flooded and no school is held.

Nov 6th 1882 Ellen Stuckey a 1 Standard girl commenced duties as monitress in place of Mrs Smith for a few weeks.

Nov 22nd 1882 Mrs Baker called to say that Herbert, her son, came to school the day before without her consent and she was afraid that she could not afford to let him come after this week.

1883

Mar 20th 1883 Mrs Michael Hale called and used language far from choice and also threatened the monitress with violence. She is well known in the parish for her foul language.

Apr 23rd 1883 Robert Norris fell in the water at 1.50 and was sent home. He came back at 2.05 so I allowed to attend.

Sep 17th 1883 Bert Scribbins appears to be suffering from scarlet fever. I thought it best to send his sisters home till Dr. Hurd gave his opinion to the complaint.

Sep 24th 1883 On Friday afternoon Dr. Hurd again saw Bertie Scribbins and reported that it is scarletina he is suffering from. Neither of his sisters can be allowed to attend. There are now one or two fresh cases, Ruth Bailey and Evyline Blanche Scribbins.

Oct 2nd 1883 There are 13 girls and 3 boys away ill this week.

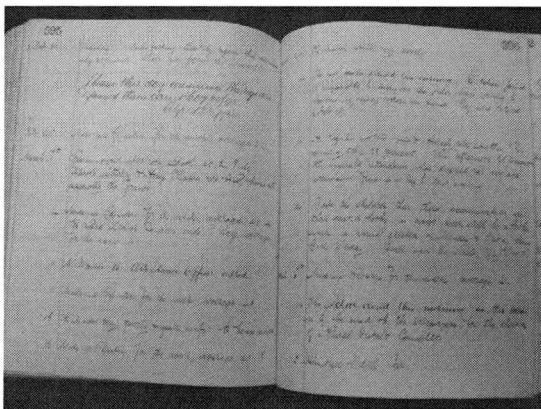

Log showing Mr Smith's handwriting

Oct 11th 1883 Albert Hale having the chicken-pox I sent his brother and sister home. Mr Gould reports that Albert Hale has scarletina. The school ought really to be closed for a week or two.

Oct 12th 1883 Dr. Hurd ordered this evening to close the school for a time.
(17 days later the school recommences).

Oct 31st 1883 Small school to-day as several of the children have gone to Yatton to spend their savings from the club.

1884

July 9th 1884 The annual school treat given by the Rector was held to-day. The children were driven in wagons kindly lent by Mr Charles Griffin to Yatton Station and taken by train to Burnham. Tea was provided for them in the Puzzle Gardens after which they amused themselves in the sands. Mrs Piggott with her well-known kindness supplying the children with small buckets and spades.

Burnham was left at 8.30 and all reached home at 10.30 delighted with their treat.

Sep 5th 1884   Mr Gage is payed (sic) for pauper children for quarter ended June 20[th.]

Sept 21st 1884 Mrs Piggott kindly sent a load of stones for the school yard where they were badly needed.

Oct 2nd 1884   Closed registers to-day at 1.30 as several of the children are going to tea at Church House.

Nov 18th 1884   The Squire's hounds meet in the village this morning, in consequence there is a poor attendance.

1885

Dec 8th 1885 North Somerset Election to-day. Half-holiday this afternoon to enable the Master to go to vote with the Rector.

1886

Mar 26th 1886 James Williams was very impertinent to the Master this afternoon when spoken to about the habit he has of keeping a dirty nose. A. Williams left to attend a private school.

Apr 5th 1886 William Fletcher a boy in standard 4 commenced bird scaring. His parents only to keep him away a fortnight.

Apr 12th 1886 Edith Neath, a sixth standard girl has left school to help her mother at home with shirt making.

Aug 18th 1886 No school to-day on account of the North Somerset Agricultural Show held in Yatton.

Nov 17th 1886   James Williams again very insolent. When punished he made use of bad language to the Master. The Rector then sent for, came, and having spoken to the boy, advised the Master to give him a good whipping.

1887

Mar 16th 1887 Heavy snow storm. Snow 16 inches deep. One boy only at school. He was sent home and school closed for a week.

June 7th 1887 No school held this afternoon as the room has to be decorated and prepared for the dinner to-morrow given in honour of the Queens Jubilee.

June 8th 1887 Closed school to-day for the above mentioned reason.

Sept 19th 1887 No school held this afternoon as so many of the children are gone to a harvest festival at Kenn.

1888

June 5th 1888 A committee meeting this evening when it was found that the school account was overdrawn to the extent of £10.1sh. Several farmers refused to subscribe. It was determined to form a Board.
Note: The 1870 Education Act had created a new type of local authority, the school board, to provide and run schools wherever they were needed. Boards had authority to draw on the rates for money to do this.

Sept 26th 1888 A meeting of subscribers took place to-night. The Rector in the chair, the Lord of the Manor also being present. Several landowners who were present gave donations to make up the balance due on last year's accounts and also increased their subscriptions as also did some of the farmers present. The Squires Piggott and Griffin and Mr John Denmead joined the committee.

Oct 2nd 1888 A small attendance this afternoon on account of a Blue Ribbon Tea.
Note: Taking the Blue Ribbon was a symbol of joining the Temperance Movement.

1889

Feb 20th 1889 Mr Tipper called. He called Mrs Parsley who disputes of her little girl. Enquiries will be made as to the right age.

May 10th 1889 The average has much improved during the last two weeks no doubt owing to the fact that each child who has been to school ten times each week will now get a ticket each Friday the same to count towards a prize to be given in April next.

Sept 10th 1889 Mrs Coombs and Mrs Scribbins having called over their children. The former has taken her 3 children from here and sent the 2 youngest to a Dame School recently opened in the Parish.

1890

Feb 19th 1890 The School opens this morning. Both Neaths on Doctor's orders away as they have Russian influenza, he says. Blanche Scribbens away, very unwell, also 2 or 3 others through fear. This being a short week, the Master will collect no fees.

Oct 20th 1890 A very small school to-day, only 19 present this morning and 17 this afternoon. Several away poorly evidently through continually finding apples, others picking blackberries, among the latter, Tommy Colbourne.

An early picture of the Rectory, the figure looking over the wall with the dog is thought to be the Reverend G.H Smyth-Piggott.

Back from left Mr Smith Thomas Fletcher Willie Traves Bertie Scribbins Ernest Hale
Harry Neath Albert Coombs James Waygood Lizzie Hale
Middle Maria Waygood Jenny Neath Florrie Hale Julia Scribbins Louey Tilly
Lily Webber Frances Cobern Blanch Scribbins Tom Cobern Herbert Scribbins
Front Eliza Coomes Flo Webber Lily Parsley Ernest Parsley Christopher Hale
Sidney Cobern   Lizzie Gardiner Willie Smith Jane Neath Mrs Smith and Baby Gertie.
May 1888

Back from left John Beedel Willie Smith Cliff Jones Walter
Stuckey Ernest Tucker George Cox Tom Summers George Neath
Mr Smith
Middle Harry Scribbins Ethel Scribbins Mabel Webber
Annie Summers Annie Fowler Flo Webber Sarah Gardiner
Winnie Jones
Front Daisy Webber Beatrice Eglinton Beatrice Gardner
Gertie Smith Alice Fowler Charlie Scribbins Frank Neath
Harry Cox Harold Stuckey
December 1894

Dec 1st 1892   A very wet day, consequently there is poor attendance.

Dec 6th 1892   The Master very unwell and feeling quite unfit to be in school.

Dec 15th 1892   Brushed Standard IV up in Compound, Multiplication and Long Division and did not follow the Timetables in consequence.

Dec 19th 1892   Lily Parsley who has been absent from school for three weeks with a scalded foot returned this morning.

1893

Jan 1893   9th Re-opened school this morning only 20 present. Afternoon school will now begin at 2 pm. instead of 1.30 pm as fixed on Nov 21st.

Feb 1893 20th A list of irregular children sent to Mr Tipper among them being Lilly Baker, Bert Jones and Beatrice Young, the latter having had her name sent in a dozen times and been away twenty three weeks.

Feb 1893 23rd Took the children for their weekly examination this morning. Made up registers for the week, average for the same 36.

Mar 3rd 1893   No school today, the Master being too unwell. The third School Quarter ends today.

Apr 27th 1893   Ethel, Harry, and Charles Scribbins were very poorly at school yesterday. This morning the parents called in the Doctor who certifies that they are suffering from Scarlet Fever. In consequence Herbert must also remain at home.

Charles Scribbins was the youngest of five children. He started work as an errand boy in the Kingston Post Office Stores and then became a grocery apprentice in Clevedon. Finally, he became proprietor of the village Post Office Stores for twenty-two years, retiring in 1958.

Apr 28th 1893   Two or three of the children are away today, the parents feeling scared at the dread of infection.

May 3rd 1893   The two Jones' are without doubt suffering from Scarlet Fever.

May 5th 1893   Received a circular from Dr Adams, the Medical Officer, saying Winnie Jones is suffering from Scarlet Fever and that the brothers must not attend school for the present.

May 11th 1893   Christopher Hale a Standard IV boy cannot get on with his arithmetic at all, so the Master has decided to put him in Stan III for arithmetic.

May 15th 1893   The following is the report of the Diocesan Inspection held on Tuesday last.
The School is in very good order and the children are well taught. Many of the infants having been recently admitted, made the answering somewhat uneven, but the repetition was very good. The elder children did well in all their work.

May 19th 1893   A very wet morning, a small attendance in consequence. Several children wet through, a fire lit in the classroom to dry their garments.

May 22nd 1893   Whit Monday. A whole Holiday.

May 23rd 1893   The Drawing Lesson taken today instead of yesterday, as the Drawing Examination is on Friday.

May 26th 1893   The Drawing Inspection by Lieut. Col. Archer.

May 30th 1893   Christopher Hale away very poorly, supposed to be suffering from Scarlet Fever.

May 31st 1893   Chris Hale died at six this morning.
The three Edwards' and Harry Howe away, the parents feeling afraid to send them for fear of infection.

June 5th 1893   Closed school today by order of the Medical Officer for the Bedminster Union, Dr. G.Adams.

July 17th 1893   Re-opened School this morning. Re-admitted Beatrice and Sarah Young and Joseph Payne.

July 24th 1893 Mrs Smith too ill to take sewing this week being confined to her bed.

July 27th 1893 Made up registers for the week, average 46.

Aug 7th 1893 Annie Summers, Gertie Smith, Elsie Gage and Walter Gage received prizes for regular attendance, the books being the gift of the master. Walter Gage came every time the school was open during the year ending May 31st 93. His sister only missed once.

Aug 10th 1893 The Grant from the Dept. of Science and Art received - the sum being 18/-.

Aug 16th 1893 The N.S.A.S. Show at Clevedon today. Small attendance at school this morning, a half-holiday this afternoon.

Report of Annual Inspection.
The order is satisfactory and the elementary work has improved, but the higher Grant for the English is recommended with much hesitation even when due allowance is made for the sickness which has recently prevailed. In other respects the school is in a fair state of efficiency. The Infants class is slightly better than last year but the reading is still weak and the object lessons are unsatisfactory. The Classroom is below the minimum size required by rule 7 (a) of Schedule XII of the Code.

Aug 23rd 1893 Grant from Education Dept. received.
As the Master wished to leave early this afternoon school began at 1.30 instead of 2.0.

Aug 25th 1893 I have this day inspected the Registers and found all correct.
> *G.H. Smyth-Pigott*
> *Chairman of Managers.*

Sept 8th 1893 A List of irregular scholars sent to Mr Tipper and a strongly worded letter concerning the same.

Sept 11th 1893 Visited the school. J.Bould. Assist. to H.M.I.

Sept 20th 1893 Small attendance this morning. It being Kenn Harvest Festival and many of the children going there this afternoon, no school will be held then.

Sept 25th 1893 Mrs Smith not in school to-day being compelled to go to Bristol about a new stove.

Sept 26th 1893   Afternoon school will begin at 1.00 to-day to enable the Blacksmith to fit the stove at 3.00.

Sept 27th 1893   The Blacksmith too busy to come yesterday. But intends coming if possible to-day, so afternoon school will commence at 1.30.
Ernest Hunt is too backward to do Standard I work.

Sept 28th 1893 The Blacksmith unable to find the Flue.
The Master heard hammering all the afternoon, so the children dismissed before their regular time, the noise was so great.

Oct 4th 1893 A very wet day. Many children have their dinners. In consequence afternoon school will commence at 1.30.

Oct 16th 1893   Re-admitted Lilly and Frank Meaker. A list of irregular scholars sent to Mr Tipper, although he has done nothing as regard to the last list.

Oct 19th 1893 Mr Davies, the Relieving Officer called to enquire if he could visit any irregular children. He called upon Mrs Meaker.

Oct 27th 1893   In consequence of a Concert being held in the school this evening, there will be a half-holiday this afternoon. This morning the registers will be closed at 9 and school dismissed at 11 o' clock.

Nov 13th 1893 From this date till the New Year, the Registers will be closed in the afternoon at 1.35 to enable the children to reach home before dark.

Nov 20th 1893 Alice Waygood and Lilly Clements came in at 2.10 a message sent to their mother.

Nov 21st 1893 The two children mentioned above again came late, arriving at 1.50.

Nov 23rd 1893 No school will be held this afternoon as the room has to be prepared for a concert this evening. Mr Davies the Attendance Officer called this morning and promised to call on Mr Edwards and Mr Hunt and see them about the irregular attendance of their children.

Nov 27th 1893 Arthur Edwards returned to school today after eleven weeks. Several away with severe colds.

Nov 29th 1893 No sewing taken today. Mrs Smith having gone to Yatton to visit one of the scholars who is ill with inflammation of the lungs.

Oct 30th 1893 Mr Davies, School attendance officer, called today and promised to write to the parents of Herbert Scribbins, Bertie Jones, George Cox and Harry Howe about their irregular attendance.

Dec 1st 1893 The Second School Quarter ends today, average for the week 37.7, average for quarter 39.

Dec 4th - 7th Master feeling very unwell and quite unfit to be in school.

Dec 10th 1893 The Master suffering from influenza and unable to get up. By order of the Doctor school closed for the holidays as he says the Master must on no account venture out of doors for two or three weeks for fear of pneumonia setting in.

1894

Jan 8th 1894 Recommence school, only 28 present.

Jan 15th 1874 Lilly Baker returned to school after an absence of 7 weeks.

Feb 1st 1894 No school held this afternoon as the room has to be prepared for a concert this evening.

Feb 7th 1894 Ash Wednesday. Registers marked at 9.5 to enable children to attend Church at 11 o'clock.

I have examined the registers and found them correct.
Alfred Griffin Feb 19th 1894

Feb 26th 1894 Admitted Blanche Webber who is on a visit to her Aunts.

Mar 2nd 1894 Made up Registers for the week, average 44.
School Quarter ends today, average for same 40.3.

Mar 6th 1894 Mrs Smith not in school this afternoon, having gone to Bristol to purchase a few things which are badly needed in school.

Mar 7th 1894 Received a parcel of School Stationery, Copy Books, Foolscap paper, pencils etc.

As several of the children intend going to a Wild Beast Show in Yatton at 5.00, the Master decided to close the Registers at 1.30 to enable them to leave in time, as otherwise they will remain away for the half day.

The Smiths

June 6th 1894 The Rector's mother and sisters visited the school this afternoon.

June 12th 1894 This morning the registers were closed at 9.5 to enable the afternoon's attendance to be marked at 11 o'clock, as Mrs GO Smyth-Pigott is going to give the children tea at four o'clock.

Oct 5th 1894 Three of the Hunts and two of the Meakers came at 2.50 this afternoon when the Master declined to admit them.

Oct 10th 1894 Lilly Paroley placed in Stan III for Arithmetic as the Master found it utterly impossible to work her in Stan IV. She seems to have no memory at all.

1895

Jan 29th 1895 A heavy snow storm, very few at school, so the Master decided not to keep them.

Feb 22nd 1895 Clevedon Petty Sessions Attendance Summons. Mr Hunt fined 1/- for each of three children, Mr Meaker fined 1/- for each of two children & Mrs Colbourne's, adjourned for two months

Note: During 1895 some of the children admitted were May Griffin, William & Wallace Studley, Beatrice Morris, Alfred Neath, Edith and Amy Phippen, Lilly Eglington, Julie Parsons, Stanley Griffin, Elsie Phippen, Walter Smith, Stanley Lewis, Elsie Stuckey, Edith Gardener, and George Woodman.

Nov 7th 1897 A very wet morning, only 27 present, Alice Neath, the Monitor, gave the Master notice that she will cease to act as such, as her mother is removing to Horsecastle, Yatton. The Master's son, Willie, who is in the Stan VII will take her place as no other boy or girl is suitable.

1896

Jan 6th 1896 Recommenced school today. Admitted four brothers Albert, Howard, William and Arthur Kingcott.

Jan 21st 1896 Mrs Smith away this afternoon having gone to Congresbury to take the children there at Swedish Drill.
Note: Swedish Drill was a popular exercise routine for which there was no need for bars, ropes etc. This seems totally unnecessary as most rural children of that period walked so far to school each day.

During 1896 some other children admitted were Philip Jones, Margaret Young, Walter Smith, Polly, Annie and Willie Jones, Lionel Summers, Fred Stockham, Ethel Baker, Alice Colbourne, Ann Davey, Rosina Willard, and Albert Gregory,

July 9th 1896 A very small attendance this morning. The children were to be taken to Sea Wall Farm (if fine) to tea, by the Master, and told to come this morning if it was likely to be wet. Though showery only 19 came. No school this afternoon as the children are going to the sea to have tea.

Oct 8th 1896 A small school this morning in consequence of a flood in the parish, some of the roads being impassable, the result of the seawall having broken down. Commenced fires.

Oct 22nd 1896 This morning Beatrice Gardner was allowed to go home at 10.15, as her mother was in a fit and a chance message reached the master to that effect. Her attendance was of course cancelled.

1897

Feb 8th 1897 C Baker & Walter Smith here this morning a plain proof that Mr Davis woke up their parents. Neither have attended since the Nov 25th.

Mar 15th 1897 The room cleaned this afternoon for an inquest to be held at 2.30 the Coroner's officer only gave notice 1 pm.

May 8th 1897 School closed today and tomorrow on account of 'Diamond Jubilee rejoicings' to be held in the village on the 9th.

May 10th 1897 Most of the 31 children present seem too tired and weary to do anything this morning, so I'll let them have it a little easier and not follow the timetable.

1898

May 2nd 1898 Alice Wayford appeared to be very poorly, her head aching and her face flushed. As her sister died at home last week of Typhoid Fever, I thought it best to send her home at once.

Note: Among the children admitted this year were Edith Eglington, Edith Cox, Philip & Lucy Glassenbury, Gladys May Hale, Fanny Bethel, Frank Davey, James Roper, Fred Uden, Nellie Thomas, Eveline Stuckey, Arthur Yearsley, Lionel, Lilly & Bessy Horsington

July 7th 1898 Wallace Studley away suffering from concussion of the brain. Received from an accident last evening.

Aug 8th 1898 Mr James Parsons Wallis, a member of the School Committee, and who took great interest in the school, died on Friday 29th July.

Aug 24th 1898 School closed this afternoon as the Master has been asked to act as one of the bearers at the funeral of a young farmer's wife, who died from the result of heat apoplexy

Dec 21st 1898 Mr Alfred Griffin called this morning and requested the Master to give each child present this afternoon two oranges, when they will be dismissed for the Christmas Holidays.

1899

Feb 13th 1899 Part of the Seawall was broken down yesterday by the tide and the roads are still impassable. No school held today.

Note: Among the children admitted this year were Olive Neath, Nellie Bond, Winnie Griffin, Henry Lampert, Albert Parsons, Elsie Langford, Willie Hale, James Scribbens, Herbert Stevens and Elsie Cox.

June 20th 1899 Harry Cox, while playing cricket in Mr Wallis's field at lunchtime, received a crack in the forehead from the bat, which cut into the bone. Mrs Smith had him driven to Dr Johnson who put a couple of stitches in it.

Oct 9th 1899 The two Eglingtons, who have been at Cardiff since the Midsummer holidays, returned to school.

1900

Jan 8th 1900 Re-opened school. 38 present. Admitted Willie Holly.

Jan 9th 1900 Admitted Florence Gratham.

Jan 15th 1900 Admitted Elizabeth Cook, who has not attended Yatton School (her last) since October.

Jan 22nd 1900 Re-admitted Harry Parsons.

Jan 26th 1900 Made up the registers for the week average 42.5.
The weather during the last two days has been very wet & the attendance poor. Many of the children have very bad coughs & so has the Master.

Feb 2nd 1900 Snow falling this morning only 26 present.
No school will be held this afternoon as it does not seem worth while bringing them back through the snow.

Feb 9th 1900 The average for week is only 32.8. It is really disheartening to see so many away.

Feb 16th 1900 School again closed only 3 children came. The roads in places impassable owing to being flooded. Average 38.

Feb 26th 1900 The two Bakers returned to school today they have been absent for 5 weeks.

Mar 12th 1900 Winnie Griffin, who has only attended one week since Oct 11th last, and Elsie & Eveline Stuckey, who have not attended since Jan 26th, returned to school today.

Mar 23rd 1900 Charles and James Scribbins left the school this afternoon.

Mar 26th 1900 Admitted Fred & Hartley Griffin and Willie and George Wallis.
Hartley Griffin was to be a conscientious objector during the First World War but tragically died in 1919 of influenza. The hymn board in the church is dedicated to him and reads:
To the Glory of God and in Memory
of Edwin Hartley Griffin 1st Scout Master.
Entered into rest Feb 11th 1919.
Presented by the boys.
Be Prepared.

Apr 23rd 1900 Re-opened school this morning. 39 present.
Admitted Dorothy Webber and Wallice Jones. The Master refused admission to Charles Scribbens as his sister has Measles, and also Beatrice Baker, because her sister, a Stan II girl, has scarletina.

Apr 25th 1900 Admitted John Lampert.

Apr 27th 1900 The carpenter here putting up fencing round the yard, the same paid for out of the V. Aid Grant.
Made up registers for the week, average 46.

May 10th 1900 *Visited of Inspection II 846*
T.H. Cooke
The playground requires to be levelled and regravelled.
A map of Europe is urgently needed.
THC
A half holiday is given in honour of the visit of Mr Cook.

May 17th 1900 During the dinner hour the Master rode down to the house of Mr Godfrey with Mr Davies, to measure the distance from the school to it.

May 21st 1900 A Whole holiday given today in honour of the relief of "Mafeking".

June 5th 1900 Re-opened school this morning. Admitted Dennis Burdge. A meeting of the School Committee held this evening, when the School Accounts were made up & Form 1X filled in.

June 20th 1900 The Diocesan Examination held this afternoon. Notice of it sent to H.M. Inspector on May 26th.

44

22^(nd) June 1900 Report of the Diocesan Inspector.
"The School seems to be in very good order and the written work & knowledge of the Bible is to be commended. The repetition is rather too fast & somewhat indistinct.

Report of H.M. Inspector for year ending May 31/1900
The work of this little school is carried on with regularity and method.
The children behave well and much of their work is of satisfactory quality although they do not answer questions so readily as they should do. The attention of the School Attendance Committee should be at once called to one or two cases of non attendance.
C. Smith is continued under Art 68 of the code.
     Alfred Griffin   Correspondent.

June 29th 1900 Made up Registers for the week, average 52.4.
Messrs H Cook and Edward Neath fined for the irregular attendance of their children. The former Five Shillings and the latter Two and Sixpence.

July 9th 1900 The reward Books given to the most regular children for the year ending May 30th.
Three were also given for proficiency in Scripture. They were given by the Master.

July 16th 1900 Willie Hale returned to school to-day. He has been absent through illness since June 6th.

July 17th 1900 Notice sent of the closure of the school on Tuesday the 24th, on the occasion of the School Treat.

Aug 20th 1900 Re-opened School this morning. 51 present.
Admitted Victor Naish and Mabel Lampert. Mrs Smith away from school, she being in Bristol nursing her son who is ill with measles. The Master's daughter will take the Infants.

Aug 22nd 1900 Mrs Smith home today, but thinks it would be wrong to come into school. The Master's daughter very poorly.

Aug 28th 1900 The Master's daughter is now suffering from Measles.

Sep 17th 1900   Willie & George Wallis have left the parish and school. The Master's daughter has also returned to her work in school this week.

Sep 24th 1900 Admitted Joseph Cox.

Sep 28th 1900 Made up registers for the week, average 50.9.
Several of the children are occasionally kept away to pick blackberries which they sell. A list of irregular children sent to Mr Davies to day.
Oct 24th 1900 School closed this afternoon to enable the Master to attend the funeral of the late Miss Griffiths, of the National Infants School Clevedon, who was a very old friend. Impossible to follow the Timetable.

IN MEMORY OF
SYDNEY JOHN HALE
OF THIS PARISH,
PRIVATE 2ND BATTALION GRENADIER GUARDS,
WHO DIED IN THE SERVICE OF HIS COUNTRY,
AT LEMBE
OCTOBER 19TH 1944 AGED 28 YEARS.
SOUTH AFRICAN WAR 1899, 1902.

Sydney John Hale was brought up in Kingston and was presumably a pupil at the school from around onwards He fought in the Boer War and died at Lembe on the th October As a schoolgirl Louise Wallis Kingcott remembered a contingent of soldiers coming from Clevedon on the Weston Clevedon and Portishead Railway to Ham Lane Halt and marching up Ham Lane to the church The memorial service and sacrifice of Sydney is commemorated in the plaque near the church door

Oct 31st 1900 Admitted Leonard Hale.

Nov 16th 1900 The weather during the whole of the present week has been very wet, the attendance has dropped in consequence the average being only 41.8.

Nov 28th 1900   A very wet day, very poor attendance in consequence.

Dec 3rd 1900 Frank Gabriel returned today, having been away a month, with an attack of measles.

Dec 10th 1900 Admitted Charles and Henry Tutton.

Dec 11th 1900 Mrs Smith away in Bristol to day, having gone with Miss Henri, to buy toys for the "Christmas Tree". Miss Henri kindly paying for them.

Dec 14th 1900 Made up the Registers for the week, average 53.5. The approaching tea is evidently an inducement to the children's attendance.

Dec 17th 1900 Winnie Griffin and Louise Wallis promoted from the Infants room to Standard 1.
Louise Wallis (later Kingcott) recalled her early years at the school in a recorded conversation with Ken Stuckey in 1983. She went to school from Cherry Tree Farm. Edith her younger sister wanted to go to school with her but was not allowed to until she was four.
'Old Mr Smith was Headmaster – Lesley Griffin's grandfather – Mr Smith's brother was headmaster of Congresbury school. His wife and daughter used to teach us music. Will Smith the son didn't help but went into printing. Old Mr Smith died quite young and might have had heart trouble, he'd very often get a faint at school and his wife had to take him outside for some fresh air to recover and then he'd come back in again. Pretty strict those old men were, they had to be, they didn't mind using the cane!'

1901

Jan 21st 1901 Re-opened School today. Should have re-opened on the 7th but closed by order of Dr Fuller Medical Officer of Health, as so many of the children had Measles.
29 present this morning. No sewing will be taken this afternoon as so few girls are present. Admitted Reggie Tutton.

Jan 28th 1901 A very wet rough morning, only 22 present.

Jan 29th 1901 Admitted Cuthbert Stuckey.

Feb 1st 1901 I have this day examined the Registers and found them correct.   Alfred Griffin Correspondent

Feb 7th 1901   Messrs A & E Griffin, members of the School Committee visited the school this morning to decide about the drainage work to be done.

Feb 11th 1901 Five of the six Joneses returned to school, they have been absent since Christmas.

Feb 16th 1901   Received some coal & coke for the school on Saturday.

Feb 18th 1901 Received a large parcel of stationery. Many of the children have very bad coughs.

Feb 25th 1901 Wandered from the timetable a little this morning. The master very unwell. Admitted John Young.

Mar 6th 1901 A very wet day, only 25 present. Most of them very wet.

Mar 8th 1901 This afternoon, by accident, the Master entered the number of girls present (18) in the boys' Register.
Mr Davies promised the Master yesterday to visit Mrs Neath and Tutton, about the irregular attendance of their children.
Made up the Registers for the week, average 36.5
The weather the whole week has been very bad.

Mar 15th 1901 Made up the Registers for the week, average 52.8. The Tuttons left this week as they are removing to the top of Yatton.

Mar 18th 1901 Admitted Gertrude, Emily & Reginald Holly who formerly attended Kenn School.

The Master and his wife both very unwell, & under the doctor, neither up to work.

Several of the scholars have very bad coughs through the bitter east winds.

Threshing at Cherry Tree Farm. From left: Bill Travis Mr Luff Mr Corfield Teddy Griffin Tom Simmons. C. 1910 (Ray Naish collection).

Mar 25th 1901 The weather very cold accompanied by snow, a poor attendance.

The Master and his wife still very unwell & not up to work.

Apr 1st 1901 Men at work to day at the drains

Apr 3rd 1901 Gave the children an examination in their Records Books. Standard I and II doing their work on sheets of paper. Those who are away will do theirs when they return to school after Easter.

Apr 15th 1901 Re opened this morning, 54 present, admitted Madge Webber.

Apr 23rd 1901 Admitted Rose Loveridge.

May 6th 1901 Admitted Maud Tucker.

May 8th 1901 Miss Seap (Lady Guardian) called to see Willie Holly this afternoon on matters connected with his application for admission to the Gt Western Railways Orphanage.

Master suffering from loss of voice.

May 14th 1901 Admitted Ada & Maud Parker.

16th V.O.I. Inspection 11 846
Fireguards are needed for both rooms. J.H.Cooke

The sum of £16.0.0 Aid Grant was awarded the School Managers on August 24th last for following purpose.
Drainage & Repairing W.C. £10
Blackboards, Easel & Repairing Harmonium £3
Books and Stationery £3

May 16th 1901 The usual holiday in honour of H.M.I will be given tomorrow. To give the Master's voice a rest, he decided to give the whole days holiday. Made up the registers for the week, average 60.9.

June 4th 1901 Admitted Charles Parker.

June 19th 1901 Admitted Christianna Laura Stuckey.

July 1st 1901 Admitted Frank Lampert and re admitted Percy Fry.
Report of the Rev.H Vaughan (Rural Dean) on Religious Knowledge,
The School is in very good order, and the children bright and intelligent. The Infants repeated very well what they had learnt, and the older children both in their written work as well as in their answering, acquitted themselves well.

Jul 6th 1901 The Annual Report from H.M Inspector received as follows:
The children are taught with care and very fair success. Illustrations should be provided for the Object Lessons.
C Smith is continued under Art 68 of the code.
Alfred Griffin Correspondent

Aug 12th 1901 Re opened School this morning, 57 present.
Admitted Lilian Mary Avery. The Room scrubbed last week.
A new cash book and slates bought. Mr G Jones fined 7/6 on a school attendance summons.

Aug 21st 1901 No school today on account of the school treat taking place at Clevedon.

Sep 9th 1901 Mrs Smith and her daughter out of school today. Both ill. The Doctor called in to the latter.

Sept 10th 1901 The Doctor says to-day, that the Master's daughter is suffering from Scarlet Fever, and ordered the school to be closed.
Notice of closing sent to C.H.B. Elliot Esq.

Sept 30th 1901 Re-opened School this morning, the Medical Officer having given permission.

Oct 7th 1901 Admitted Daisy Dixon. Aid Grant to the amount of £16 has been granted for the following purposes. Improvement of School Yard and Well £12. Stove and Grate £4.

Oct 25th 1901 Maggie Young's name sent in to Mr Towell for irregular attendance. Eight names sent in to Mr Davies for the same cause, some of the boys are attending very badly.

Oct 30th 1901 A note received from the correspondent (Mr Griffin) saying that Mr Pitts' price for a new grate for the Master's house and a new stove & guards for the School had been accepted. Mr Pitts has been asked to do the work at once.

Nov 8th 1901 Visited with Mr Aldis, Chief Inspector.
H.W. Irvine Head of Schools.

List of Object Lessons for Stan 1-VI
The land; Woodland; Meadowland; Ploughland; Moorland.
Working Roots and creeping roots. Roots, their structure and work.
Stems; Woody stems; Climbing stems.
Tubers (The potato). Seeds; Method of distribution.
The Mole; The Hedgehog; Common Snake (compared with viper).
Garden snail; The earth worm.
Paws & Claws & their uses. Tails and their uses. Tongues and their uses.
Hair; Fur; Wool and their uses. Beaks of birds and their uses.
Water; how carried. Things that dissolve. Things that melt.
Water; Manufacture of salt from brine.

Nov 14th 1901 Mr Davies called today.
New grate for the Master's house and the new stove for the classroom brought to-day.

Nov 21st 1901 Men in to put up the stove in classroom, all the children had to work in the large room.

Nov 22nd 1901 Stove not finished so must all work in the large room again, this overcrowds us. Mrs Smith not in this afternoon, as she is in the house cleaning up the mess made by the masons. Shall not follow Timetable in consequence. Made up registers for the week average 57.

Dec 3rd 1901 Mrs Smith away having been called by telephone to see her mother who is dying.

Dec 4th 1901 Mrs Smith having lost her mother by death will not be in school again this week. The Master suffering from a severe cold.

1902

Jan 6th 1902 Re-opened School this morning 51 present. New fire guards put up on Saturday last.

Jan 15th 1902 The Master suffering a bad bilious attack and not fit to be in School, consequently it was not opened.

Jan 16th 1902 A very poor attendance this morning, the evident result of closing yesterday.

Jan 17th 1902 Mr Neath summoned to attend Clevedon Petty sessions on Friday next, on account of the irregular attendance of his son Frank.

Jan 21st 1902 Many of the children are suffering from very bad coughs and colds.

Feb 3rd 1902 Maggie Young returned to school after an absence of six weeks.

Feb 14th 1902 Elsie Cox is suffering from ringworm in her head, the master told her brother to tell his parents to keep her home and have it seen to. The Master called upon Colour Sergt Baber of Yatton to see him about coming to drill the children.

Feb 19th 1902 Sergt Baber came and gave the children their first lesson this morning.

Feb 26th 1902 Mrs Smith too poorly to be in school this afternoon, no sewing in consequence.

Mar 14th 1902 Mrs Smith away this afternoon, having gone to visit Barton Hill Board School (Girls) Bristol, to see some demonstration sewing lessons with Miss Smith of Congresbury National School.

Mar 17th 1902 William Cox sent home as his head and neck have several ringworms upon them.

Apr 21st 1902   A very wet morning with poor attendance, 39 present. Admitted Fred Burdge.

Apr 28th 1902   The Master very unwell and quite unfit to be at work. Mrs Smith too has lost her voice through cold. The Master has been under the Doctor since Easter Tuesday.

June 2nd 1902   Mr A Griffin, the secretary, gave the children a half holiday, in honour of the Declaration of Peace with the Boers.

June 17th 1902   The Coronation Festival of His Majesty is to be held in the parish tomorrow. On that account school will be closed for the remainder of the week and also the whole of next week

Thursday 26th June 1902
The following is a copy of the Report of H.M. Inspector of Schools:
The School is in very good order and the children carefully taught. Some provision should be made to improve the ventilation.
Alfred Griffin Correspondent.

June 30th 1902   During the holiday a bell, kindly given by Mr John Wallis, was to have been put up over the classroom window, in honour of his Majesty's Coronation. Owing to illness the work has been stopped. The bottom seat in the classroom was broken by falling stone and though Mr Pitts was requested and promised to put in a new one, it has not been done.

For sixty six years the bell hung on the outer surface of the west gable of the school.
John Wallis (died in 1905 aged 72 years), whose family had lived and farmed in the village for many generations, found the bell when it was washed up on the seashore. It must have been in a wooden frame which would have given it buoyancy. Bob Ford remembers that 'as children we were told it was a ship's bell. It seems this was not so because the bell is plain with no markings whatsoever. It was probably from a bell buoy which had broken away from its moorings. It called my father, myself, my older son and a host of others to the classroom.'
After the school closed in 1968 and the building was sold the bell was passed back to the village and in 1979 was re-hung in the village hall where it remains.

The first entry for the School Managers meeting book is as follows:-
A meeting of the Managers of Kingston Seamoor (sic) School was held on the evening of July 7th /902
Those present Col. Long, C.M.G. Messrs A Griffin, E Griffin, F Stuckey, W Burdge & H Price.
It was proposed by Col Long and seconded by Mr E Griffin, that Mr Alfred Griffin be Chairman and Correspondent of the Managers.
Col. Long proposed that the amended claim for salary of the Master, be sent in to the County Education Committee.
Alfred Griffin (Chairman)

Aug 27th 1902   A whole holiday given to day, as many of the children are going to the Coronation Festival at Horsecastle, a part of Yatton.

List of Object Lessons for Stan1-V1 for year ending Midsummer 1903

A Farmyard	Bread
Work in the fields in the Summer	The Birds and their Nests
	Sheep
Water and Uses	The seasons
The Farmer's Pests	Crops grown and their uses
The Garden Snail	A River, its banks, birds and animals that live near it
Bees	
A Mill, The Miller and his Work	Animals on a Farm
	Migrating birds

An Apple Tree	Trees
Caterpillars	The Cow
Harvesting	A Railway
A Plough and other	The Hare and Rabbit
implements on a farm	A Newspaper
A Dairy	

Sept 5th 1902   Form 17 A (V.S.) from the Education Department says £22 has been granted for the following purposes.

1. Fencing & Pointing front of school	13.0.0
2.Shelter in Playground	5.0.0
3.New Desks and pictures for object lessons	4.0.0
	22.0.0

Nov 10th 1902 The Master ill and unable to open school.

Nov 12th 1902 The Doctor ordered the Master two weeks rest at least.

1903

Jan 5th 1903   Re-opened school. Being wet morning only 35 present.
Admitted John Wallis, Thomas Flower, James Flower & Hilda Flower in the afternoon.

Feb 10th 1903 The Shelter in the Yard commenced by Mr Pitts of Congresbury.

Feb 23rd 1903 The Master suffering from a severe cold, quite unfit to be in school, will be bound to take things quietly. Ethel Baker, a Stand V girl, died of consumption yesterday. Her mother died 3 weeks ago of the same complaint.

Feb 25th 1903   No sewing this afternoon, Mrs Smith having gone to Bristol to buy a wreath, subscribed for by the children to be placed upon Ethel Baker's grave.

Apr 20th 1903 Re-opened school this morning. Admitted Doris, Edwin and Harold Ford who have never been to school before.

May 5th 1903   A very wet morning, a fire lighted and the children's clothes dried in the classroom.

July 4th 1903 The following is a copy of the Report of H.M.I.
This little school continues to be taught with care and success. The use of slates is objectionable.
School Staff: James Smith (Master)
(Mrs) Clara Smith   Art 68
Clara Gertrude Smith

> *The Managers' estimates of expenditure 1903 – 1904 included the salary for James Smith as £94-5-6, a recommendation that Mrs Smith now receive a salary of say £30 (as she had previously not been paid) and that Miss Smith now being 18 would have a pay rise from £2-10-0 to £10 per year. Gertrude Holly the school cleaner was due to receive £2-10-0 pa.*

Sept 2nd 1903 A very wet day, yet 60 present, nearly 50 with their dinners. In consequence, we will re-open afternoon school at 1.15 and dismiss at 3.25.

Sept 4th 1903 A parcel of drapery, food arrived from London for school use.

Sept 16th 1903 Received from Mr Alfred Griffin, a new Minute Book, Stock Book and Punishment Book.

Sept 17th 1903 Received by rail from London, a supply of Exercise Books VC to the order of the County Education Committee.
Half a hundred tiles sent for repairing the roof damage in the gale last week.

Nov 3rd 1903 Frosty morning. Fires made in both rooms and will be continued in the mornings at least.

Nov 23rd 1903 John Tombs, an infant scholar, who was at school up to Thursday afternoon last, died last evening of Diphtheria. Lilly Lampert, another infant, very sick in school this afternoon.

> *Dec 1903 Extract from School Managers' Meeting: The late gale removed several tiles from the Master's house and the roof of the Schoolroom, which I have replaced, I have also had 50 tiles of another pattern to replace them, not being able to obtain any to match the old ones. I think the whole expense will be under £1.*

1904

Jan 19th 1904 Re-admitted Ethel Avery.

Jan 25th 1904 Re-admitted Fred Pearce. The Rev. H. Vaughan, Rural Dean, called in this afternoon.

Feb 15th 1904 Daisy Webber was away this morning, and I thought this afternoon, so marked her absent. After closing time I found her present so marked her so.

Mar 21st 1904 Admitted Arthur Parsons.

Apr 12th 1904 Admitted F.W. Cleverdon.

May 9th 1904 A map of Europe, new Geographical Readers, new Registers, Records Books arrived.

May 31st 1904 The school year ends today average attendance 58.86.

June 7th 1904 Revd J Mather, Vicar of Yatton, called this afternoon. He was accompanied by his daughter.

June 13th 1904 Admitted Elsie A Tucker.

June 20th 1904 Admitted Albert Godfrey and E Jowles.

July 22nd 1904 The Master away for quarter of an hour, in the churchyard, attending the funeral of Miss Smyth-Pigott, sister of the Rector. Mrs Smith in charge during that time.

Sept 8th 1904 Mr Davies, the attendance officer called in today, when the master reported non attendance of Percy Lampert, who was reported by the Master, as not attending school some three months ago. He went down to the mother, who promised he shall attend next Monday. His attention was also called to Phillip Jones, Walter Smith and Ernest Norris who have not attended for the last two weeks.

Sept 12th 1904 Admitted Walter, Mary and Gilbert Goodliff.

Sept 13th 1904 Admitted Percy and Annie Lampert.

Sept 14th 1904 Alfred Neath came this afternoon at 1.45 and was sent home at once.

Oct 6th 1904   The three Goodliffs came in this morning after the Registers were closed.

Oct 21st 1904 Mr Alfred Griffin distributed prizes given by the County Education Committee, to the 16 most regular scholars in the Standards V and IV in the Infants Class.

Mr Smith and Miss Gertie Smith pictured with pupils. Victor Naish is standing next to Miss Smith while Alf Neath is sitting in the front row on the right.

Oct 24th 1904   The three Goodliffs came in this morning at 10.7. Miss Mather, a member of the Yatton Attendance Committee, called this morning. Prebendary Vaughan, Rural Dean, called this afternoon.

Nov 14th 1904   Admitted Ada and Ernest Neath and Wilfred Lampert.

Nov 4th 1904   Mr D. Davies called in today and reported that Messrs Waygood and Goodliff were to be summoned for the irregular attendance of their children. Made up the Registers for the week, average 52.

Nov 24th 1904   A half holiday this afternoon to prepare the room for a concert.

1905

Jan 9th 1905 Lionel Summers presented with silver medal for four and a half years regular attendance. It was engraved with his initials and recorded his attendance.

Jan 23rd 1905 Admitted Harry Norris.

Jan 25th 1905 The cess pool emptied.

Feb 8th 1905 Admitted Cecil Ford.

Mar 3rd 1905   The Master and his wife summoned to a Commission of Enquiry by the Lord Bishop, into the conduct of the Rector (Rev. George Herbert Smyth-Pigott) the said enquiry to be held in Yatton.   No school held in consequence. Average attendance for the week 51.

Note; the Commission was held in the Assembly Rooms Yatton, The court was headed by the Archdeacon of Bath. The charges against the rector was his neglect in regularly performing divine services and his lack of reverence, also his neglect of visiting the ill and poor and his neglect in the instruction of the young in the catechism. The church was said to be practically empty during services sometimes with only two or three people present. The organ keyboard lid was nailed down, the bells were not rung and the church was full of mildew and damp. There were no acting churchwardens at the time and the sexton had not been paid.

Alfred Griffin of Riverside Farm said that a lot of the trouble dated back to the school management row, he had written to the Bishop nine years previously concerning the poor state of affairs. James Smith the schoolmaster said that he had stopped attending the church because the last time he was there the rector laughed nearly the whole time during the service. The Rev Smyth Pigott himself attributed the falling off in the church to the school incident in November 1902 'the row was about Smith allowing some of his scholars to teach in his absence, and he (the rector) objected to it. A meeting was held and he (the rector) was voted out and ever since then there had been a coolness between Smith and himself'. Many parishioners gave evidence against the rector.

His first wife had died at an early age and his subsequent marriage to his parlour maid had caused much disapproval in the neighbourhood. He stated in the enquiry that the marriage had taken place in a registry office. After leaving Kingston Seymour, following the court, the rector moved away and eventually died in 1929 at Bournemouth.

Information from the Clevedon Mercury and Courier March 1905.

Mar 24th 1905 The Bishop, having inhibited the Rector from performing the ecclesiastical duties of the Parish, has appointed the Rev. M. R. R. Green as Curate in Charge. This gentleman visited the school with Mr. Alfred Griffin this afternoon.

Chapter 6
The Edwardian School

May 2nd 1905 Mr. Wake of Messrs Wake and Dean called about the repairs to the Master's Desk, promised to send for it tomorrow. Rev. Green (Curate in Charge) called this afternoon.
Rev. Green was paid a small stipend as Curate-in-Charge, he was also employed as a Church of England Schools Inspector.

May 15th 1905 Admitted Bertie Saunders and Beatrice Cox.

May 16th 1905 Admitted Gillian Baker.

May 23rd 1905 Admitted Doris & Ginnie Body.

May 25th 1905 A letter written to Messrs. Wake and Dean, asking them to send me the Master's Desk and New Cupboard as soon as possible. Both the above received this evening.

July 11th 1905 The Diocesan Examination held this morning. A half holiday in the afternoon.

July12th 1905 Form for a Summons filled up for Alf Neath.

July 21st 1905 The parents of Alice Young and Alfred Neath fined at Clevedon for their irregular attendance.

July 28th 1905 This morning at 12, dismissed the children for their Midsummer Holidays of 4 weeks. School will re-open on Monday Aug 28th.

> *Extract from School Managers Meeting 10th October:*
> *Deeds of School placed into the Wilts and Dorset Banking Co., Clevedon Branch, the sum of £20-0-0 on deposit, in the name of the Curate in Charge and the Church Wardens.*

Sept 18th 1905 Admitted Annie Parsley.

Sept 25th 1905 Re-admitted Doris Ford.

Oct 5th 1905 Mr D Davies called respecting the attendance of Alfred Neath, Gladys Hale and John Eglinton.

Oct 20th 1905 Mrs Dean, Miss Sybil Long, and a lady friend, came into school this afternoon. The two former are daughters of Colonel Long C.M.G.

Nov 3rd 1905 A half holiday given to the children this afternoon, for making 90 per cent attendance for the last four weeks.

Nov 27th 1905 Mary & Jack Plumley admitted. A note sent about the Neaths to Mr Davies.

1906

Jan 8th 1906 Re-opened school this morning, 61 present. For the future, will in the mornings, mark those present by 9.5 in red ink, as Managers and the Master have promised a reward to a few of the children who attend earliest.

Jan 9th 1906 Admitted Edgar Hunt aged 5.

Feb 22nd 1906 This morning I found that the three Cleverdons have chicken-pox though the parents reported the case as a cold, Arthur Parsons too has it.

Feb 26th 1906 Admitted Gertrude Hunt.

Feb 27th 1906 Mr Ford sent to say that Cecil is covered with a thick rash this morning, so as the other three were in school, I sent them home. Norah Webber who was very poorly at school yesterday, was away this morning suffering I imagine from chicken-pox. Mr. Cleverdon called last evening to see if he could send his boys to school. I was out, but will write and request him to keep them home the remainder of the week.

Feb 28th 1906 This morning Mr. Neath sent a note to say Letitia has chicken-pox, and would keep Olive and Annie away for a few days. Norah Webber is at school this morning and seems quite well.

Mar 1st 1906 Mrs. J. Wallis sent to say Edith and John both have chicken-pox this morning. Gertrude Stuckey is away with it, and the two sisters Body are ill. Gladys Hale, I have just heard, has it as well.

Mar 2nd 1906 Two fresh cases of chicken-pox reported this morning.

Mar 5ᵗʰ 1906   A reply received on Saturday morning from Dr. Fuller, in answer to a letter I wrote to him on Thursday, asking if he thought we should close for a few days. He said, "If the attendance continues to drop, I could get a certificate from the local Medical Man." His reply sent to Mr. Bothamley, and a request, "As to what I had better do in the circumstances."

Mar 6ᵗʰ 1906   Reply from Mr. Bothamley received this morning, saying, "No need to close."

Apr 2ⁿᵈ 1906   Last Monday morning, Mrs. O. Lampert called to say she was leaving Kingston, and the children would not be coming again. This morning all four returned to school again.

Apr 25ᵗʰ 1906   The Venerable the Archdeacon of Bath and the Rev. M.R. Green visited school this afternoon.

May 21ˢᵗ 1906   Admitted Alan Sweet and Bertie Saunders.

Jul 20ᵗʰ 1906 The Diocesan Inspection took place today. Children dismissed for the Summer Vacation for four weeks, re-opening Aug 20ᵗʰ

Report of E.S.Mostyn Pryce.
Handwriting may be praised. In Arithmetic the style and neatness of figuring would perhaps improve if slates, which are in occasional use up to the top of the school, were given up. The Oral subjects may also be improved in intelligence, especially the Geography, if there were a written syllabus of instruction and by means of more practice in answering in complete sentences instead of single words.
The Infants seem to be progressing fairly as far as can be judged in the absence of any written year's syllabus of their work.
Singing is fair and discipline is good.
A full detailed year's scheme of work should be prepared both for the elder scholars and for the Infants and the quarterly work should be entered in the record books before each quarter begins.
Staff: James Smith   (Master)
Clara Smith   Art 68
Clara Gertrude Smith   (U)
Alfred Griffin   Correspondent

Aug 29th 1906 A whole holiday to day on account of the 'Harvest Home' being held.

Oct 19th 1906 Made up Registers for the week, average attendance 59. William Cox and Thomas Eglinton fined 5/- each and Edward Neath 4/- for the irregular attendance of their children.

Nov 2nd 1906 A load of coal and some wood ordered for the school fire.

Nov 5th 1906 The Rev. Irvine, Vicar of East Clevedon and the Rev. R.J. Ives, of St. German's, Roath, Cardiff, visited the school this afternoon, and remained some time.

Nov 28th 1906 The Master very poorly, the Rev. M. R. Green took the Scripture lessons. Shall not follow the Timetable.

Nov 29th 1906 The whole holiday today and the children will be given a tea in honour of Miss Smith, 21st birthday. Miss Smith given a travelling trunk by the Managers, and a toilet set and case by the children.
The managers presented her with a handsome leather travelling trunk and the children a leather toilet set and case, with the following address: " We the children of the Kingston Seymour School, cannot let your 21st birthday pass without showing our deep regard and love for you and we therefore ask your acceptance of the accompanying toilet case, not for its value, but simply to express our love and appreciation for the many kindnesses we have experienced at your hands. Hoping that you may be spared many years to work in the school and that the future may bring much happiness." The senior scholar Edith Eglington presented the toilet case, after which hearty cheers were given.
Extract from the local paper

Note: Edmund Eglinton was the younger brother of Edith and was born in 1902. He later wrote an excellent book called *The Last of the Sailing Coasters* which was published by the National Maritime Museum in 1982. Edmund's father was the contractor on the construction work of building the sea walls in the early 1900s. He describes how in 1910 stones from nearby quarries were brought in by ship to the river Yeo. He and Edith – then 15 years old - had to light a beacon in the dark so that the incoming trow could navigate to the river. The following morning one of the men carried him over the mud to the boat and this was the first time he had ever been aboard a ship. He was allowed to leave the village school in 1916 to go to work on the walls as labour was scarce during the war years and the sea defences were considered important. Edmund sailed in these ketches and trows, engaged in local trade in the Bristol Channel, until the early 1930s.

Dec 4th 1906   This morning every child on the Register was present.

Dec 14th 1906 Mr William Cox fined 5/- and 4/- costs and Olive Lampert 2/6 for the irregular attendance of their sons Wilfred Cox and Harry Lampert at Clevedon Petty Sessions today.

1907

Jan 7th 1907 Reopened school 55 present. Admitted Wallace Hale.

Jan 22nd 1907 A very cold and wet morning, only 35 children present. 49 present yesterday morning, when it was thick fog. I am not surprised at the number away as so many have bad, Influenza colds.

Mar 2nd 1907 A meeting of the managers held today. Several children who are away are reported to have Whooping Cough.

Report of H.M. Inspector on the visit of the 12th.
...The Infants are taught with fair results. The Infants room measures only 15 feet by nine feet and is more than half filled by the gallery. The ventilation in this room is unsatisfactory.
There is not a lavatory.
Alfred Griffin Febry 28 1907, Correspondent.

Mar 14th 1907 The Rev. M.R. Green in this afternoon, and heard the children receive a Sol Fa lesson and sing their songs. Many of the children have very bad coughs.

Mar 21st 1907 Many of the children at school have Whooping Cough. Mr Davies the Attendance Officer, called in Dr J.P. Johnson who said we should close. He ordered Mr Davies to write and lay the matter before Dr. Fuller, Medical Officer of the Union.

Mar 25th 1907 Closed for four weeks on account of Whooping Cough, by order of Dr Fuller, Medical Officer of Health to the Long Ashton Local Board.

Apr 22nd 1907 Re-opened school today, 33 present.
Admitted Charles and Lizzie Hawkins and Elsie Flowers.

Apr 25ᵗʰ 1907   A letter sent to Mr Lye the Clevedon Attendant Officer asking him to look up the Youngs who are away, and to order the attendance of Polly Young, who is about 5 yrs old, and whose name was sent to him some three months ago.

Apr 29ᵗʰ 1907   Fifteen present today, who were away last week. Admitted Polly Young and Elsie Parsons.

May 1ˢᵗ 1907   Wrote to Mr I Davies, asking him to look up the Hales, of North End. Sent an absentee form to Mr F Sweet.
Made up the registers for the week, average attendance 54.

May 6ᵗʰ 1907   The Hales and Alan Sweet, who had not attended since March 22ⁿᵈ came this morning.

> *Extract from School Managers Meeting 8ᵗʰ May 1907:*
> *Mr Needham of Yatton to price the connection of a Lavatory for Infants to be fixed to the girls lobby.*

June 3ʳᵈ 1907   Admitted Dorothy Grace Hale.

Aug 26ᵗʰ 1907   Re opened school this morning 49 present.
Admitted Bernard Griffin and Reginald Stuckey.

Reg Stuckey in recorded conversation with Ken Stuckey in 1983 recalled his school years: "I never went to school much, too much work to do. I started when I was 6 year old, on my 6ᵗʰ birthday milking a cow, cow's name were Lily, and been at it ever since. When I was 9 I'd go out milking with a pair of yokes, milk 5 or 6 cows myself, carry it home. While I was having my breakfast, I'd put milk up in a cart and take the milk over to the milk factory at Kenn – Stowells – on my own, then go to school. Eleven years old when I had to leave school for it was the First World War and Father was left on his own. I was the eldest boy. I was very pleased at the time but have seen the folly of it since."
Reg was brought up at Rustic Farm and was one of six children.

Aug 29ᵗʰ 1907   A very bad attendance to day, in consequence of a tea, to which several of our North End children are invited, beginning with games at 2 pm.

Jan 7th 1908   Re-opened school after Christmas Vacation. 43 present, a very wet morning. Admitted Stanley Plumbley and Stanley Towzer.

Jan 10th 1908 The attendance during the week has again been very bad, so many have still the breaking out on the face and head.
Average attendance 50.

Feb 1st 1908 School Piano arrived to-day.

Feb 3rd 1908 Reggie Flowers who has been at work since the Christmas holidays (though not qualified to leave) compelled to attend. Came in this morning. Rev. M.R. Green visited school this afternoon.

Feb 10th 1908 Re- admitted Dorothy Hale.

Mar 5th 1908 Report of A B Fisher Esq:
...The Infants are taught in an ill ventilated room measuring only 15 feet by 9 feet. More than half the floor space is occupied by an unnecessary gallery.

Mar 9th 1908 Admitted Alice Pyke.

> *Extract form School Managers Meeting 9th March 1908:*
> *As regards the Infants classroom, the Gallery complained of will be removed during the Easter Holidays. The correspondent was instructed to see and make arrangements with Mr W Traves as to taking out of the above but was not able to form an estimate as to the cost of moving, to being unable to see the state of the floor under.*

Mar 30th 1908 Admitted Fanny Godfrey.

Apr 6th 1908 Admitted Marshall, Reggie, Cicely, and John Clark.

Apr 27th 1908 Re-opened school this morning. Mrs Smith too ill to be in school and under the Doctor. Admitted Harold Cleverdon.

May 1st 1908 Admitted Richard Sweet. Mrs Smith returned to her school duties this morning.

May 5th 1908 Admitted Kathleen Webber. Rev M. R. Green in this afternoon.

May 19th 1908 This morning 64 children were present, so thought it best to give them an examination in their Records Books, which I accordingly did.

May 25th 1908   The Committee decided that the children be granted a half holiday this afternoon it being Empire Day. Last Friday Mr Goodliffe was fined 5/- for the irregular attendance of May, his daughter.

June 15th 1908   Admitted Fred Scribbins, Frank Clarke, Agnes Ford and Alice May Norton.

July 22nd 1908   Miss Smith away this morning, having gone to Clevedon to prepare her stall for the Church Bazaar this afternoon in aid of the Church Restoration Fund. A half   holiday in consequence of the same.

Aug 26th 1908   Admitted Florence Watts.

Aug 27th 1908   Admitted William and Ethel Crook, who say that they are come on a visit of two months, with Mrs Pyke.

Oct 5th 1908 Medical Inspection of the children by Dr. Stevenson, some of the children detained till 12.45, Miss Smith also.
No Sewing taken this afternoon.

Oct 26th 1908   The Rev. M. R. Green visited the School this morning and remained some time.
The four Hales came again this morning after 3 wks absence, owing to measles, also the two Pykes.

Dec 14th 1908 Admitted Edith Fletcher.

Dec 18th 1908   Richard Sweet no 28 on the infants Register has been away poorly for two days. I glanced round his class and did not notice him, but marked him absent for the day, as he lives 2 ½ miles from here (*presumably Sea Wall Farm on the back road to Clevedon*) and he always brings his dinner. On marking up the registers and counting those present, I found he was here, so I marked him present and will do so again this afternoon.
Average attendance for the week 63.8

Dec 23rd 1908 Dismissed the children for the Christmas Holidays.
Rev. M. R. Green came in this afternoon and distributed the prizes given by the County Council for Regular Attendance.

1909

Jan 18th 1909 Re-admitted Alice Norton.

Jan 25th 1909 Admitted Violet Fletcher.

Jan 29th 1909 Report made by H.M.Inspector J B Russell Esq.
After visit of Dec 11/908
Premises
  1 The Playground is not in good condition. It should be levelled in places and gravelled.
  11 Some Apex ventilation is desirable in the classroom.
  111 The premises need painting, colouring Etc.

Work
Mixed
1 The general education standard reached has improved during the year. It admits however, of much further improvement.
2 The subjects still needing attention are Grammar, Geography, Arithmetic in the Upper and reading in the Lower Division, where it is lacking in fluency.
Handwriting generally is praiseworthy. Better material should be supplied for the making of garments.
3 The proportion of the whole school of the children working in classes corresponding to the old standard 3 to 6 is not very satisfactory, but it does not appear that any faulty organisation accounts for this disproportion.
Infants
1 The Infants are taught in a kindly way, and in the formal subjects their attainments are satisfactory.
2 The very small classroom was overcrowded on the day of inspection; 21 children being seated in nine dual desks. It is understood that the number of children has now been reduced to 16. Since, however, the room is only nine feet wide, it is clear that the accommodation is not suitable (Art 18 of the code). Enlargement of the classroom is much needed, in order to give a sufficient amount of space for the teaching of those subjects specially requiring free movements.
3 The Scheme of work should be drawn up on a more methodical plan.

  Alfred Griffin Correspondent.

Feb 8th 1909 Admitted Laura Pearce.

Feb 20th 1909 Dr Bendle of Bath, examined a score of scholars this afternoon.

Mar 8th 1909 A holiday given to day, in consequence of a visit to the parish by the Lord Bishop.

Mar 30th 1909 Admitted Reginald Herbert and Gladys May Bessant. Alice Pyke away with Chicken Pox, and her sister Lena is ordered by Dr Johnson to remain away as well. He has also ordered Alice Norton to remain away for two weeks as her little brother has Chicken Pox.

Apr 19th 1909 Re-opened school after the Easter Vacation. Admitted Harold Simmons, Elsie Watts and Henry Hale.

June 18th 1909 Made up Registers for the week, average attendance 59.1. Percentage of attendance 97.

> *Extract from School Managers Meeting 10th August*
> *Mr Taylor Architect for the proposed addition to Infants Classroom, explained plans approved by Board of Education. Mr Taylor to invite tenders as soon as possible. 24th August... The tender of Mr E H Coles be accepted for the sum £130 (other quotes – W King £135, W Hill £149-10-0).*

Aug 31st 1909 The children attending the nonconformist Sunday Schools here and at Horsecastle, are away for a treat, a very small school in consequence, 41 present. Rev. M.R. Green came in.

Sept 2nd 1909 Miss Henly, Instructress of Cooking, visited the school this morning concerning the children who intend going to the class in Clevedon.

Sept 6th 1909 The work of enlarging the classroom commenced to day. Three men commenced taking down the front wall and throwing the stone into yard, dangerous to the children.

Sept 24th 1909 Men are breaking into the classroom from the boys lobby, have removed the stove, it is very dirty and dusty and the noise very annoying. The girls unable to wash their fingers since having their dinners, so sewing cannot be taken.
Decided to close school till Wednesday Oct 6th.

Oct 25th 1909 Found impossible to re-open till this morning. 53 present. All working in the large room. Admitted Richard Bessant.

Oct 26th 1909 A very wet and cold day, a great change in the weather. Started fire in the large room.
The yard in a very bad state through the heaps of refuse left by the workmen, which is brought in on the children's feet.

Nov 1st 1909 Re-admitted Frank Clark. The classroom unfinished, all working in the large room. Impossible to follow Timetable.

Nov 11th 1909 Taken bad when marking the Registers, and made a wrong entry at foot of Infants Register. The total was 12 but I entered 19 twice.

> *Extract from School Managers Meeting 18th Nov:*
> *Permission given to Mr T W Phippen for use of the Schoolroom for a dance in aid of School Building Fund.*

Dec 2nd 1909 A Sale of Work is to be held in the school tomorrow (Friday) in consequence there will be no school.

1910

Jan 11th 1910 The Webbers have had a sister home from service with measles. Yesterday morning I sent the infant Kathleen home, and wrote to Dr Bendle, Bath, about them.
In afternoon I saw signs of the complaint upon Norah's face, so told them not to come to-day.
Elsie Cox was very poorly in school yesterday afternoon, and her brother Joe this morning. Mrs Cox has this morning sent a note, to say they are too poorly to come, and are very giddy.

Jan 28th 1910 Mary Holley away, supposed to be suffering from Measles. Only 46 present this morning.

> *Extract School Managers Meeting 11th Feb:*
> *The Correspondent reported that after paying all bills in connection with the additional building to Classroom there remained a balance in the Bank of £12-10-0. A rough sketch was presented for the New Offices for boys & girls. Mr Taylor asked to get out plans & acquire tenders.*

Feb 14th 1910 Received notice that May Goodliffe and Gilbert Goodliffe had removed to Kenn and were going to school there.

The Webbers still away, so I sent the Regulations in account of Infectious Diseases to Mrs Webber.

Feb 15th 1910 Mrs Webber came to say she would not yet send her children to school. This afternoon Mr Hayward called to promise to call upon Mrs Webber.

Mar 14th 1910 Admitted Gladys Young. The Pykes have left, having removed to Yatton.

Gladys Young (one of 10 children) was born at Burnt House down across the fields from Riverside farm (the cottage is gone now). She had to walk from the cottage down past Riverside to the school. In the company of her husband Ted Parsons she recalled her early school days in conversation with Ken Stuckey in 1983:
"Very often when the Baker did call Mother did say, Have you seen my little girl coming home? And he'd say, she's out in the middle of the field with the sheep all round her – fast asleep!"
Ted milked cows by hand at Cherry Tree Farm for Mr Wallis before going on to school.

Mar 24th 1910 The Medical Examination held this morning. The Doctor ordered Hilda, Evaline, and Dorothy Hale home, as they had dirty heads. Their attendances were crossed off in consequence. Made up the Registers for the week – average 57.2. Dismissed the children for the Easter Vacation.

Apr 4th 1910 Re-opened school this morning. Admitted Stanley Cleverdon and Frank Plumley. 60 present.

Apr 8th 1910 No Sewing taken this afternoon, neither is Miss Smith in school, as she is in the house, the paperhangers being busy there.

Extract from School Managers Meeting 8th August
The new lavatories to be deferred.

Aug 24th 1910 No school today owing to Harvest Home.

Aug 31st 1910 Nine children away this afternoon, they attend the Chapel Sunday School, and thought they were going to Weston for their school treat, but it is raining again, so they will not go till the next fine Wednesday afternoon.

Sep 1st 1910 Miss Gatehouse, the Instructress of Cookery, called this afternoon, to see about the girls who are to attend the class at Clevedon.

Sep 5th 1910 12 children away this afternoon having gone to Weston for a treat connected with the Chapel Sunday School.

Dec 5th 1910 The Nurse did not visit on the 30th Nov, but have just had notice she will come at 3 o'clock this afternoon.

Dec 8th 1910 Received notice from Dr Savage. County School Medical Officer, to exclude Winnie & Polly Young and John & Agnes Ford from school, so sent all four home. The Fords had their notice yesterday, but came this morning.

Dec 16th 1910 At 3 o'clock this afternoon Mr Baker called, to say he must have his child Lilly, as his wife was taken ill, and he wanted her to look after the children.

1911

Jan 25th 1911 Sent letter to the Chairman of the School Attendance Committee, complaining of the continued bad attendance of Mabel Lampert.

Feb 6th 1911 Admitted Frank Griffin.

Feb 17th 1911 Rev. M. R. Green came in this morning. Olive Lampert fined Five shillings for bad attendance of Mabel.

Mar 6th 1911 Annie Parsley taken poorly in school this afternoon & sent home. Dr Johnson reports her to be suffering from consumption.

Mar 8th 1911 Admitted Arthur Vivian Ford.

Mar 29th 1911 Wilfred Hale away suffering from blood poisoning, he was at school till the 23rd.

Apr 4th 1911 Harold Simmons met with a sad accident last evening having been thrown from and also kicked by a pony. H S was taken to Bristol Hospital.

Apr 5th 1911 Harold Simmons has a fractured skull.

Apr 12th 1911 Elsie Sweet, Edward Parsons & Arthur Ford, crying & complaining of headache. Arthur Ford who had his dinner at school, had to go home at one o'clock.

Apr 24th 1911 During the holidays the four Plumbleys removed to Chew Magna.

May 4th 1911 Miss Smith covered with a thick rash. I have sent for Dr Johnson & she will remain in the house. Telegraphed to Dr Savage.

May 5th 1911 Closed school for two weeks, by order of Dr Savage, as Miss Smith is suffering from Measles, caught through sitting next to a young lady at the Yatton Teachers Class who had just recovered from an attack.

> *Extract from School Managers Meeting 11th May*
> *Discussed the best means of making the Offices in a more sanitary condition. It was proposed and seconded that arrangements be allowed to stand over for a short time to see what money would be in hand. Tenders asked for the enlargement of the West window in the schoolroom.*
> *Mr A Griffin resigning his position as correspondent at end of school year May 31st.*

May 26th 1911
Made up the Registers for the week – average 51.9. Admitted two girls & boy during the week.

In signing this book after having acted as correspondent for the past 18 years, I return my most sincere thanks to Mr & Mrs Smith for their kindness, courtesy & assistance during the time I have acted in that capacity.
Alfred Griffin May 31st/11

June 1st 1911 Visited the school found all satisfactory & listed Registers
M. R. Green, Correspondent.

> *Extract from Managers Meeting: Tenders for painting lighting and heating for the interior of the School also lowering the window at the West end of the schoolroom and putting in two skylights in the roof on Southside 36 x 42 ins.*

June 13th 1911 The Coronation Festival in the Parish will take place tomorrow, in consequence of which, the school will be closed for the rest of the week. Average attendance for the week 52.

June 19th 1911 Re-opened school this morning. Admitted Hilda May Sweet.

June 27th 1911 Dr Parker held an examination of some of the children this morning. Fred Badman's mother took him away with her at 11.10 so I marked his attendance off.

July 20th 1911 The Diocesan Examination was fixed for tomorrow, but the Rev. Preb. Vaughan by mistake came in this morning so held it to-day instead.
The children were then dismissed for their Four Weeks Holiday, during which the school window at the end is to be lowered, and the rooms painted inside.

Aug 28th 1911 Re-opened school this morning, we should have done so last Monday but the work was not near completion.
Admitted Ernest Norton & Arthur Hale.

Extract from a letter to Joan Ridley from Mr Stanley Cleverdon, Sept 2003:

I left Kingston School when I was 6 years old so remember very little about it. What I do remember is the teachers, Mr Smith, Mrs Smith and Miss Smith. I also remember the window in the large schoolroom being enlarged due to some regulations. It must have been a hot summer for when we returned from the holidays Mr Smith put blackboards over the new part of the window as it made the room too hot!

My family lived at Hope Farm, Kingston Bridge, for about 10 years. I was the youngest of 6 children, all boys. My eldest brother, aged 17, was drowned while bathing at Kingston Seymour. My mother was so upset we had to leave Hope Farm. For six months we lived at Cherry Tree Farm next to the School. Then the family moved to Claverham where my mother lived for 50 years. On the whole they were happy days at Hope Farm and at the school. I remember the children of the families who lived there, the Travises, the Wallises and the Griffins.

There was a most severe drought in the summer of 1911 and drinking water for the animals was in short supply. The rhynes dried up and farmers had to dig holes down through the mud in the rhynes to find some water. Other farmers took their animals out of Kingston to the bow at North End where there was a river. Mr Harold Stuckey drove his father's animals to Tynings farm on the Mendips for pasture he had rented there. After driving them all that way he then had to walk back. Grass was so sparse that some farmers cut elm and withie leaves for fodder.

On Sunday 20th August, a very hot day, a terrible tragedy occurred. Teenagers John Cleverdon and Lionel Summers went down to Kingston sea wall. The walls were about 30 yards further out from the present bank. They walked out across the mud to a sand bank at low tide, the tide came in and they were cut off before they were aware of it. John Cleverdon could not swim and Lionel, who could, ran to the village for help. There were no boats nearby and by the time rescuers got there with ropes, it was impossible to save him.

Sept 5th 1911 Edward Parsons who was present yesterday, has measles.

Sept 18th 1911 Allan Sweet, Edgar Wallis, Eveline Hale, Polly Young & Lily Stuckey who were at school on Friday are now reported as having Measles.

Sept 21st 1911 Eveline & Dorothy Hale came in again this morning not having had measles, as reported on Monday.

Oct 2nd 1911 Commenced fires in classroom.

Oct 24th 1911 This afternoon at 3.15 Arthur Hale, an infant asked leave to run out, not coming back. I sent a boy out and we found he had run off home. I crossed his attendance off.

Nov 6th 1911 Admitted Charles Young.

Dec 6th 1911 The School Nurse visited this morning, and inspected some of the children's heads.

Dec 21st 1911 This afternoon the children were awarded their papers for regular attendance & dismissed for the Christmas Vacation. School will re open on the 8th of Jan.

24th Dec 1911 Extract from Managers Meeting: Mr WSAW Travis appointed in place of Mr A Griffin (resigned). The fee for use of schoolroom 5/-.

1912

Jan 8th 1912 Re-opened school this morning 47 present. Admitted Susannah May Cox.

Jan 17th 1912 Visited the school and tested Register found all satisfactory.
M. R. Green , Manager.

Jan 18th 1912 The County Council Nurse came in this morning, but the girls she wished to see were away. This morning we had a heavy fall of snow, a small attendance in consequence. At 12 o'clock it is still snowing, so we will not open this afternoon.

Feb 1st 1912 A half holiday this afternoon, in consequence of Choir Outing.

Feb 2nd 1912 Philip & Christopher Glastenbury have not attended since Dec 21st both are infants. The father was leaving his place of work and going to Brean, I was told, so they were marked off the Register. Last Saturday the Rev. M. R. Green informed me they were still in the Parish, but suffering from Whooping Cough, so I re-entered their names.

Feb 13th 1912 Reggie Clark who has been absent since Sept 12th was forced in today.

Feb 19th 1912 Received Medical Certificate for Annie Parsley.

Mar 1st 1912 Made up Registers for the week, average 45.4

Mar 6th 1912 Beatrice Cox came in this morning, but is still far from well.

Mar 13th 1912 Cecil Ford came in this morning, but looks very ill.

Mar 18th 1912 Mrs Webber sent to say her two little girls have sore throats, and a medical certificate will follow.

Mar 21st 1912 Received a Certificate Form from Dr Fuller, reporting, Gertrude, Lillian, Reginald, Arthur & Frank Stuckey, and Kathleen & Winifred Webber to be suffering from Infectious sore throats.

Mar 25th 1912 The school drains stopped up, Walter Baker opened them.

Mar 27th 1912 Eveline Hale very poorly this afternoon at 3.10 so sent her home and her attendance crossed off.

Mar 29th 1912 Made up Registers for the week, average 33.2. The four Hales left during the week.

Apr 2nd 1912 Admitted Ethel Clark

Apr 4th 1912 Tomorrow being Good Friday, we close the afternoon and re-open again on Monday April 15th.

Apr 15th 1912 Re-opened this morning, with much better attendance, 43 being present. Admitted Bertha May Luff, who is nearly six but has never been to school before. Several being away, sent off to Mr Hayward at once.

Apr 23rd 1912 The Master being very unwell, did not take drawing this afternoon.

Through illness of Headmaster.
School was closed from April 23rd to May 8th.
M. R. Green, Correspondent

> *Extract from School Managers Meeting 10th May 1912:*
> *Letter of sympathy sent to Mrs Smith, on the death of late*
> *Mr. Smith, Schoolmaster for 29 years.*

Extract from local paper (presumably Clevedon Mercury):
It is with infinite regret that we have to announce the death, on Wednesday, of Mr James Smith, who, had he lived another month would have completed thirty years service as school master of this parish. The deceased gentleman, who was 57 years of age, had been actively engaged in his professional duties until Friday last,

but on the following day he became indisposed, pneumonia set in, and, despite devoted nursing and the best medical attention, his strength gradually failed death resulting from heart failure. His passing has evoked a sense of mourning which is not merely confined to the parish wherein he had so faithfully and fruitfully laboured, but is shared by residents in a widely extending area, for the deceased was held in unqualified respect and regard by all who possessed his acquaintance... Particularly will his association with the Church Restoration Fund be recalled, for, as befitting a loyal son of the Church, he worked with a self devotion and zeal which brought in hundreds of pounds for the carrying out of a scheme which transformed a sadly-neglected edifice into a comfortable and in every way seemly place of worship. Then he was also the hon. sec of the old Harvest Home Committee, and indeed of practically every social, festive or otherwise deserving parochial movement. Mr Smith was a member of the Chew Decanal School Union, and was held in high regard and respect by his colleagues in the North Somerset Branch of the National Union of Teachers.

Mrs Clara Smith was born 21st June 1855. She moved away from the village eventually and died in 1945. Both Clara and James Smith are buried in Kingston churchyard.

Their daughter Miss Clara Gertrude Smith had been born on 29th November 1885, she married Samuel Austin Griffin and they lived in Yatton and owned the West End Stores. She had one son Lesley who took over the running of the shop after the Second World War. She died in 1959.

May 8th 1912 Wednesday. Frederick James Arthur (Trained Certified Teacher) undertaken the temporary duties of this school today.

May 17th 1912 Visited School, Mr Arthur, owing to illness unable to be present. Everything otherwise satisfactory. M.R.Green Correspondent.

May 31st 1912 Last day of the School Year. Average for past year 46.

June 3rd 1912 Staff: Fred Jas. Arthur Trained certificated (on Supply), Mrs Smith supplementary, Miss C Smith.

June 3rd 1912 Polly Young returned to school today.

June 6th 1912   Thursday. Leave of absence kindly granted for this afternoon.

June 12th 1912   Wednesday. Registers not marked this morning Diocesan Examination by the Revd. Marshall. Holiday granted this afternoon.

June 14th 1912   The Diocesan Report to hand. The following is a copy:-
The children were quiet and in good order. They seemed interested in their work but very little had been prepared, only part of the Scripture Syllabus - very little Catechism and no Prayer Book. This is not satisfactory and I hope that the full syllabus will be taken in future. The writing is good and what little Repetition had been prepared was nicely said.
J G Marshall Diocesan Inspector.

June 28th 1912   Friday. A Holiday granted to day on the occasion of the King's visit to Bristol.

July 12th 1912   Children are working well and making good progress in their various subjects.

July 18th 1912   Absent from School this afternoon having to attend to private business.

July 19th 1912   My duties as Supply Teacher terminates to day after a period of eleven pleasant weeks among the children.

> *Extract from School Managers Meeting on 5th and 11th June 1912*
> *52 applications for Head & interviewed Owen, Sheppard, Turner & Maslen. W Sheppard appointed as Headmaster £81 with house, without house £90 p.a.*

Chapter 7
War Clouds

July 22nd 1912 Monday Commenced duties as Head Teacher of this School. Wm J. Sheppard (Cert'f'd).

July 29th 1912 Miss Smith absent from duties owing to indisposition (cold).

July 30th 1912 Mrs Smith is taking Stds 1 & 2 together with Infants as Miss Smith is still absent.

July 31st 1912 Miss Smith resumed duties. Attendance poor owing to heavy rain.

Aug 2nd 1912 School closed at noon for Summer Holidays.

Sept 2nd 1912 Monday. School re-opened. 52 present. Admitted Wilfred & Sidney Griffin.

Sept 9th 1912 New Time Table under consideration by Co. Committee & awaiting approval of H.M.I. Started work by it today.

Sept 11th 1912 Mr Long Co. Council Inspector visited school today.

Sept 17th 1912 Older girls at Clevedon all day (Cookery).

Sept 19th 1912 Mr Burton H.M.I. visited school to day. He remained all day.

Sept 23rd 1912 Monday. Attendance poor owing to a Sunday School Treat (Chapel).

Oct 2nd 1912 Wed. Attendance low owing to weather being wet & rough. 39 morning 45 afternoon. Commenced brushwork as the colours arrived from E.S.A.

Oct 8th 1912 Tuesday. Received suggested Arith'c Books from Scholastic Taylor. Started use of same in classes today.

Oct 9th 1912   *Visited the school, and tested Registers, found
everything satisfactory, work progressing favourably.*
M. R. Green, Correspondent.

Oct 10th 1912   Mrs Smith unwell this morning. Gave her
permission to absent herself in afternoon.

Oct 16th 1912 Wed. Nature Notes arrived – Started use of same.

Oct 18th 1912 Made up Registers – attendance good. Viz 98%
mixed & 84% Infts.

Oct 22nd 1912   A. Parsons, W Lampert, C Clark, L Baker to
Clevedon by 11.30 train for Med. Insp. Oculist – let them all out
early & gave them their attendance.

Oct 28th 1912 The Clarks (4) absent owing to heavy rain having
flooded road.

Nov 4th 1912 New Reading Bks (Press Forward Series) also Geog
Readers for upper Stds. arrived. County pastels & drawing books
to hand. Am starting work with above.

Nov 5th 1912 New cupboard from Wake & Dean to hand this
morning.

Nov 6th 1912 Wednesday. Dismissed School for mid-term holiday.
Re-open Monday 11th.

Nov 11th 1912   Managers kindly gave me permission to return
Monday by first train which necessitated my being ¾ hr late.
Several children absent owing to illness. May Luff & E Mills
(chicken pox) & A Stuckey (breaking out).

Nov 20th 1912 Received T Table approved & signed by H.M.I.

Nov 26th 1912 Attendance poor 28 mixed 12 Ifts owing to rain.

Dec 9th 1912   Mr. Hayward (Attendance Officer) called this
morning. Made out Certificate showing L. Lampert's attendance.

Dec 13th 1912 Completed examination for 2nd yr. Made out list in
order of merit & sent parents a report of each child's work. Not so
satisfactory as I could wish. Also tested Infants in Reading, Recita.,
Number and examined their writing books.

1913

Jan 6th 1913 School re-opened to day after Xmas Holidays. Kathleen & Winifred Webber gone to Yatton until mother's house is unoccupied. One or two absent with Whooping Cough.

Jan 7th 1913 Received card from Dr Savage asking for address of Lillian Baker's father re providing spectacles.

Jan 17th 1913 Admitted B Kingcott on Monday. Attendance lowered by one or two cases of Whooping Cough.

Jan 31st 1913 Ethel Clark has Whooping Cough, so sent Forms MD 1&2 To Med. Office of Health & Dr Savage respectively.

Feb 3rd 1913 Heard from Dr. Fuller Med. Off. Health saying the Clarks should all be excluded from attendance at School.

Feb 5th 1913 Hilda Sweet taken ill in School. Sent her home with her sister 11.15.

Feb 14th 1913 Made up registers. Attendance for week low, owing to exclusion of Clarks, A Parsley, E Mills also away ill. Mr Hayward (Atten. Off.) called in morning. I made him out a certificate of Hilda Hale's attendances.
The older girls finished their course of cooking lessons at Clevedon Yesterday 13 inst.

Feb 20th 1913 Received a letter from Dr Savage saying Lillian Baker would be provided with spectacles from County funds.

Mar 14th 1913 I have to day written the managers re. Mrs Smith's conduct towards myself. In front of the school she objected to my marking an examination which I had given Std 2 & which the quarter before she said she would rather I did as it would be more satisfactory. She then left her class telling me she was going to see the Rev. M. R. Green.

Mar 19th 1913 Finished final examination of the year. Sent report to each child's work to parents. Mr Hayward called & asked for Attec. Forms to be filled out for H Hale & L Lampert which I did.

Mar 20th 1913 G & C Glastenbury left village. Commenced school this afternoon at 1.20 and dismissed at 3.35.

Apr 1st 1913 Eight infants promoted to Std.1. T Ford, A Badman, E Baker admitted to infant dept.

> *Extract from Managers Minutes 3rd April 1913: An appeal made for money for the Lavatories.*

Apr 7th 1913 The Clarks return to school after an absence of 8 weeks. Mrs Hale is keeping Hilda from school as she says she has a place for her. She is not 14 nor has she made sufficient attendances.

Apr 14th 1913 H Hale resumed attendance.

Apr 21st 1913 Mr Hayward called re. H Hale's attendance.

Apr 25th 1913 Miss Russell (Organising Inspectress of Domestic Subjects) asked for nos. of girls to attend cookery class at Clevedon - 8. 2 have not yet attended a course, 3 have had one course, & three have had two courses.

Apr 29th 1913 The Nurse visited the School today & examined the heads of all the children. Notes were sent to Mrs F--- (Kate) Mrs C-- (May).

May 1st 1913 Inspector Hart (NSPCC) called today in reference to Gilbert Goodliff.

May 7th 1913 Received Labour Certif. No. 1A (for total exemption after 13 yrs of age) in respect of Arthur Parsons.

May 9th 1913 The attendance this week has been low owing to continuous rain. Dismissed School for Whitsun Holidays. Admitted B Masters, J Scribbins and Gladys Larder.

May 26th 1913 The Nurse, Miss E P Tones, visited school. Kate F and May C to be kept apart from other children (P.T.). Admitted Phyllis Sweet.

May 29th 1913 Dr Savage ordered exclusion of Agnes F, Evelyn H, Dorothy L owing to verminous condition.

May 30th 1913 End of School Year. Av. Attec. 46. Staff: Wm J Sheppard Cert (Head), Clara Smith 'S' Clara Gertrude Smith 'S' (Infts.)

Extract from Managers Minutes 9th June 1913: Donations for new lavatories – Rev. RI Ives £2-2-0, Collection Jon Sermares, Roath £7-10-0, SE Elton £5, Mrs Smyth-Pigott £10 making total £24-12-0. On 18th June 1915 a tender from Mr J A Lee £81-16-0 accepted. 31st March 1914 'Part of the garden be taken away at back for new offices'.

July 2nd 1913   Cecil Ford left this week having qualified for Exemption Certificate. Closed School Thurs & Friday 3 & 4 Royal Show & King's visit to Bristol.

July 19th 1913   School closed till Tuesday Aug 19th for Summer Holidays.

Aug 19th 1913   Re-opened School this morning. Miss Smith's notice expired on the 11 inst & Mrs Smith has leave of absence for another month. As no other teacher has been appointed, I have the whole school on my hands & consequently work is rather disorganised.

**Clara Gertrude Smith got married on the 18th of August.
The man on the right is her brother William .
(Local History Society)**

Aug 25th 1913   Miss Vivien Yelverton commenced duties here as Monitress.
At present I have placed her in charge of the infants.

Aug 27th 1913 The girls are not taking needlework for the present, as there is no teacher to give instruction.

Sept 5th 1913 Miss Yelverton has been taking needlework this week. Heavy rain all the morning lowered the attendance. Miss Yelverton could not cycle so she did not arrive till 12.00 there being no earlier train.

Nov 19th 1913 Dr Parker came for Med. Insp. 10 a.m. He remained all day. Edith P – ringworm on neck, to be excluded till better.

Nov 28th 1913 Made up Registers for the quarter. Av Attec. 48. 91%

1914

Jan 7th 1914 School re-opened to day after Xmas Holidays
Mrs. Sheppard commenced duties as Asst. teacher in the Infant Division. She will also be responsible for the needlework.
Miss Yelverton taking Stds. 1& 2.

Jan 16th 1914 Needlework to be commenced on a new scheme. Most of the girls are bringing material to make garments with.

Jan 26th 1914 Miss Yelverton came by train this morning, so did not get to school till 11.30.
Note: Presumably the late Miss Yelverton would have come from Clevedon on the Weston, Clevedon & Portishead light railway and would have alighted at Ham Lane, or Broadstone Halt. This section of the line had opened in 1897 and the railway eventually closed in 1940. According to a 1909 timetable the first train from Walton in Gordano or Clapton Road would leave at 10.45 arriving at Ham Lane Halt at 11.14am.

Mar 4th 1914 Attendance in Infants is very low (only 4 this morning & 5 afternoon). So many are away with colds & coughs.

Mar 16th 1914 Miss Yelverton late 9.40.

Mar 18th 1914 Miss Yelverton has not been to school today. Unwell.

Mar 19th 1914 Miss Yelverton late 11.30.

Mar 20th 1914 Attendance dropped owing to rain and snow. Miss Yelverton not at school today.

Mar 24th 1914 Miss Yelverton 9.40

Mar 27th 1914 Completed Examinations – sent reports to parents showing exactly what each child has done and their positions in the various classes. Admitted John & Margaret Powell, Ivy Lampert & Wm. Vowles.

The pupils in the following photograph were identified by Ken Stuckey several years ago together with the houses where they lived at the time.

First Row
Dick Sweet – Sea Wall Farm: Wilfred Lampert – Church Cottage (now a garage): Edith Parsons and May Webber - Lampley Cottages, Evelyn Hale – Prospect House, Back Lane, Ethel Clark – Sea Wall (now Mrs Blakes house), Agnes Ford – New House Farm, Alice Norton – Triangle Farm, Lilian Stuckey – Rustic Farm, Jack Powell – Moorside Farm,

Second Row
Ivor Bailey – Bridge Foot Farm, Reg Stuckey – Rustic Farm, Bernard and Reginald Griffin – Riverside Farm, Evelyn Mills – Rectory Cottage (Her father was the gardener to Rev. Green at the Rectory.), May Luff - Cherry Tree Farm (died at 12 years old), Elsie Sweet – Sea Wall Farm (Back Road to Clevedon), Fred Scribbins – Cottage in Ham Lane (now the bungalow owned by Mrs Toogood) Arthur Stuckey – Rustic Farm, Gladys Young – Cottage in Middle Lane, Winifred Webber – Lampley Cottage, Hilda Sweet – Sea Wall Farm, Margaret Powell – Moorside Farm.

Third Row
Frank Stuckey – Rustic Farm, Arthur Hale – Prospect House, Charley Young – Middle Lane, Ernest Norton – Triangle Farm, Arthur Ford – New House Farm, Edmund Eglinton – Laburnum Cottage, Ted Parsons - ? Myrtle Cottage, Wilfred Griffin – The Post Office (became Reverend Griffin), Jack Clarke – Sea Bank, Bird Griffin – The Post Office, Frank Griffin – Rookery Farm, Fred Badman – Duck Lane.

Back Dick Sweet Wilf Lampert K Webber Edith Parsons Evelyn Hale Ethel Clark
Agnes Ford Alice Norton Lillian Stuckey '?' Jack Powell Mr Sheppard standing
Middle Ivor Bailey Reg Stuckey Bernard Griffin Reg Griffin Evelyn Mills May Luff
Elsie Sweet Fred Scribbins Arthur Stuckey Gladys Young Winnifred Webber Hilda Sweet
Margaret Powell
Front Frank Stuckey Arthur Hale Charley Young Ernest Norton Arthur Ford
Edmond Eglinton Ted Parsons Wilfred Griffin Jack Clark Bird Griffin Frank Griffin
Fred Badman 1914 or 1915.

Mr Sheppard and pupils circa 1916 (Tony Bailey)

Circa 1915
Mr Sheppard with Miss Cox

(Tony Bailey)

Report of HMI Mr L D Cane visit 25 Feb 1914.
Premises: 1. The playground surface is very uneven and should be attended to without delay. 2. Both sets of offices are cramped and offensive and should be remodelled. Equipment: The desks in the main room are without backs and should be gradually replaced. Signed M. R. Green Correspondent.

Apr 6th 1914 Admitted Ivor Bailey.

Apr 27th 1914 Admitted Winifred Traves.

May 8th 1914 Miss Robinson, County Needlework Inspectress, visited the school this afternoon. She expressed satisfaction and said good progress had been made.

May 22nd 1914 Miss Yelverton late owing to puncture on the bicycle tyre.

May 27th 1914 Mr Long called this afternoon to inspect the new desks.

May 28th 1914 School Year ended 31st May. Staff: WJ Sheppard Hd Teacher, Mrs Sheppard C, Miss Yelverton M.

June 8th 1914 Re-opened School after Whitsun Holiday. Re-admitted Gladys Young & admitted Joyce Sweet, Alfred Parsons. 10 New dual desks to hand for 1st class.

June 16th 1914 The Chapel Sunday School went to Weston this afternoon – attendance therefore poor.

June 24th 1914 The School Nurse examined all the children's heads this afternoon. 57 present out of 58 – Badman being permanently absent.

July 9th 1914 Miss Yelverton away from school to-day – unwell.

July 30th 1914 Closed school this afternoon for Summer Holidays. The prizes for attendance were presented by Colonel Long and Rev. M. R. Green also said a few words.

Aug 31st 1914 Re-opened school after summer holidays. Several children absent. Admitted Rhoda Hale. Commenced work by the new Time Table.

Sep 7th 1914 Miss Yelverton 9.45. Tyre burst.

Sep 16th 1914 Miss Yelverton 9.45. Rain at Portishead.

Sep 18th 1914 Bernard Griffin absent afternoons. His father's men have enlisted so he is needed for milking till their places are filled.

Sept 23rd 1914 Miss Yelverton 9.40 puncture.

Mr Hawkins, Backwell, called. He is undertaking School Attendance Duties for Mr Hayward who is with the Army.

Sept 24th 1914 Miss Yelverton 9.30. Accident with bicycle.

Oct 1st 1914 Miss Yelverton gave notice of leaving. She has obtained a position nearer home.
Mr A Williams called at School to complain about Lesley being punished. Mr Williams is a towering rage, and dared anyone to ever punish his son. He is writing Mr Bothamly and the Managers also Mr Grey (Solicitor). I told him I should not admit Lesley again till he has arranged his terms with the above. This is the second time he has made himself objectionable.
The boy's punishment was one stroke on the hand, with a small stick, and was administered by Mrs Sheppard.

Oct 5th 1914 F Badman returned to School to day. He has been absent since Sept 14th 1913.

Oct 22nd 1914 Copy of Report of Mr Burton on visit of 9th Oct 1914.
Report of HMI Mr L Stratford
The Master had the help of a Monitress, only, from August to December 1913, and, whilst she took charge of the Infants the Master supervised her efforts and was responsible for the teaching of all the children in the standards. As a result of this arrangement – due to a temporary deficiency in the staff – the work of the school has suffered and this is especially evident in the backwardness of Stds 1 and 2. The Monitress has of late assisted the Master with the two lowest standards, but it cannot be said that the children in this class have been effectively trained in good school habits – they are deficient both in attention and diligence. The older children, on the whole, are fairly efficient in their different subjects but it is desirable that they should become more interested in schoolwork and more eager to make progress...
M. R. Green, Correspondent

Oct 30th 1914 Miss Yelverton's notice expires today. She is commencing duty at Clapton on Monday 2nd Nov.
Note: Poor Miss Yelverton's struggles to get to Kingston School on time were finally at an end! Her circumstances do show however that the railway and the bicycle had expanded people's horizons.

Nov 4th 1914 Dr Parker visited School. Impossible to do any settled work all day, as one teacher had to supervise Infants and all the Standards. Dr Parker excluded M Powell (ringworm) and she must not be readmitted without a certificate from Dr Savage. No notice must be taken of local Doctor's Certificate.

_____ excluded till 1 April 1915. Nervous. Suspected M D.

Dec 21st 1914 Miss Barbara Cox (Burrington) has been appointed Supplementary Asst. for Stds 1and 2 to commence duties on Jan 11th

1915

Jan 11th 1915 Re-opened School.
The new Offices are in course of construction; in consequence the playground is in a filthy condition.

Feb 8th 1915 Admitted Blanche and Jack Palmer.

Feb 10th 1915 Admitted A P... – she is very backward – 12 years of age in Std 2.

Feb 16th 1915 Admitted Win and Bertie Panes.

Mar 24th 1915 Reported Julia Scribbins as suffering from Mumps.

Mar 29th 1915 Phyllis Sweet Mumps. New Offices in use.

Florence Kate Ford (Kitty Bailey) and Arthur Ford.

Apr 9th 1915 Mrs Kingcott summoned for non attendance of Bertie – ordered to send him. Bernard Griffin's father called to see if Bernard could be spared afternoons as he was short of labour, owing to men enlisting.

Apr 28th 1915 Received notice from Mr Hayward (Attd Off.) to say Bernard Griffin was now temporarily exempt.

May 4th 1915 Sent forms to Mr Hayward giving the attendance of B Kingcott.

May 5th 1915 The elder girls are to attend the cookery centre on Fridays all day. This will necessitate a change in T.T. if they are to receive full instruction to needlework.

May 14th 1915 Mrs Sheppard very unwell on 12th did not come to school.

May 31st 1915 Re-opened school (Whitsun holidays).
Miss K Hill commenced duties as temporary teacher for Infants. School year ends. Av 50.

June 1st 1915 The financial School Year begins to day.

Aug 20th 1915 Several children are kept away for haymaking although the holidays were given a fortnight earlier for the haymaking.

1916

Jan 24th 1916 J Powell and B Griffin are leaving school at 11yrs and 12yrs respectively in order to work in agriculture, during the period of the war only.

Apr 7th 1916 R Stuckey and W Panes have temporary exemption from school, during war, for agriculture.

May 15th 1916 Admitted V(?) & F Cox who have come to live at Prospect Ho.

June 22nd 1916 The Headmaster away from school in order to attend Military Medical Board at Colston Hall, Bristol.

Aug 25th 1916 Attendance very poor this week. P Pople, W Brown, P & J Sweet still holidaying. W Griffin and F Scribbins away all week to assist father. 5 boys absent on agricultural work.

Aug 28th 1916 Admitted A Brown, F Trott and R Trott who are staying in village temporarily.

Aug 29th 1916 The above children left again today owing to the aunt whom they were staying with going out of her mind.
W Brown's name removed from register. He has left parish temporarily because his mother has been placed in asylum.

Oct 4th 1916 Received notice requiring me to join the colours *(i.e. his regiment)* on Tuesday Oct 17th.

Extract from School Managers Minutes:
School (to be) closed for a week's holiday from Friday 6th
Oct to 13th Oct owing to Headmaster going to colours

Note: Mrs Amy P. Sheppard was acting as temporary
Head Teacher while her husband was away, Mrs Lewis
was in charge of the Infants.

Ken Stuckey started at the school at about this time:

My education was meagre. I started school in the dark days of World War One, the headmaster had been called up, and his wife, with the help of an assistant, was struggling to teach 50 or 60 boys and girls of all ages between 5 & 14.
I learnt to write on a slate with a slate pencil. Being left-handed did not help, for they made me write with my right hand. When I moved on to a copy-book, which was the copper plate type of writing, that didn't help either for my new teacher was very handy with the thin edge of a ruler across the knuckles!

Later on, Mother wanted me to go to a private school, but Father did not agree, for he had just bought his farm and was struggling to pay for it. He said that he would educate me to become a farmer. I am glad that it went that way, for with no homework and not having to travel away to school, I was able to spend a large part of my time in the open and on leaving school before I was 14, I took my place with the regular farm workers.

School Games
We had 3 little playgrounds, the girls played in front of the school, boys in the largest one at the side and the infants had their own little space in the rear. I don't suppose many would have heard of several of the boy's games.

Lilley was very popular: the playground was oblong - which helped, for a chalk mark was drawn across it at either end. One boy started off in the middle and the rest stood at on end. The object was to get across the area without being caught and held. When you were caught, you helped the catcher in the middle. Numbers in the middle soon increased and it was a case of ganging up against the mad charges that went on from end to end until all were captured. It was then the place of the last one caught to stand alone in the 'middle'.

Lampey was another mad rush game; we started off with one 'catcher'. We had the freedom of the playground and often went into the girls' area as well. When the catcher had held someone, they held each other by the hand and endeavoured to add to their numbers. Often it was a mad rush to get away, for if the chain of hands was broken then you could not capture anyone. Even if the number of 'catchers' increased there were only two hands to hold those who were still free.

Tops were a regular; anyone could spin a top but if you could get a 'flyer' and take it around the playground or along the road in jumps of 5 or 6 yards and keep it spinning, then you were good.

Hoops, we usually got the hoop of an old cider barrel.

Marbles, often played along the road going home from school as was '<u>det</u>' or 'debt'. The proper name was 'touch' but we always knew it as 'det'. There was always rivalry between the 'up-the-roaders' and 'down-the-roaders'. Someone would 'touch' you and you in turn would endeavour to touch one of the 'up-the-roaders' and so get rid of the... call it what you like.

I must mention '<u>conkers</u>', for there was a lot of off-the-field tactics attached to this game. It was unlawful to bake a conker in the oven or use one left over from last year, as they became hard. The string they were threaded on had to be a certain length. I think it was about a foot. If possible the most suitable was an old leather boot-lace. I think everyone knows the game: you each had a conker threaded on a string and whilst one held this conker out the other one tried to smash it with three shots. If you did not succeed the process was reversed. The conker that won became a 'oner' and, as long as it remained intact, so the number of smashed ones were added to the score until it was itself smashed and the new winner took over the score. If when hitting, you missed your opponent's conker and the strings tangled you both shouted 'chops' and the first one to call got an extra knock.

Happy days indeed...

1917

June 5th 1917 Closed the school owing to chicken pox epidemic until Mon 16th .

Children admitted this year included Ronald Coles, George & Violet Evans, Norman Latham, Ronald Lampert, Florence, Edward, Gladys & Lillian Hedges, and Dennis Wallis.

1918

Jan 14th 1918   A considerable fall of snow. Number of children present 27.

Jan 17th 1918   One child sent home with wet feet.

Apr 9th 1918 May Luff left school to attend Secondary School.

Oct 23rd 1918 Lesley Williams suffering from 'Spanish Influenza'.

Nov 12th 1918   The managers very kindly gave in the afternoon a holiday to commemorate the signing of the Armistice.
A brass plaque on the church's litany desk commemorates Trooper Wilfred Pope (North Somerset Yeomanry) killed at Ypres 1914 and Corporal Reginald Holley who died at Salonica February 1918.

Dec 2nd 1918   There is an outbreak of Influenza in the village. I received notice from Dr Savage to close the school for two weeks.

1919

Jan 25th 1919 Mr Sheppard recommenced duties as Head Teacher after serving in H.M. Forces since Oct 1916, first with Household Battalion, Windsor, and then Welsh Guards.

Feb - 1919 Bad attendance owing to 'flu. Only 14 present and Infants School abandoned on recommendation of Dr Savage.

Mar 4th 1919 School closed till Mar 17th on recommendation of Dr Savage (Influenza).

Among the children admitted that year were W Vowles, Alice & Elsie Glassenbury, Mercy Scribbins, and Mervyn Griffin.

1920

May 31st 1920 Miss Kingcott of Claverham has been appointed Asst. Teacher (Supplementary).
Among the pupils admitted that year were L Parsons and E J Powell.

Sept 27th 1920 Offices in filthy state at back – not been cleaned for a week or two. Cleaner dissatisfied with rate of pay. I have this day pointed the matter out to the correspondent.
Note: a couple of days later the toilets were cleaned but whether this rare act of militancy resulted in a pay rise is not recorded.

1921

May 6th 1921   R Lampert, swinging on rafters of shed in playground, fell and broke his arm. The children have been warned repeatedly not to do this.

June 24th 1921   Received from Long Ashton District School Attendance Prize Shield this day – the school having qualified to hold it by obtaining an attendance of 95.4% for the year 1920.

Aug 31st 1921   Re-opened School. Removed M Powell's name from the register as she is recognised as P.T.C. Monitress from 1 Aug.

Nov 11th 1921 Armistice day – Marched to memorial cross – two minutes silence – Rev. M. R. Green prayers – sang "O God our Help in Ages Past" - returned to school.

1922

Jan 9th 1922 Re-opened school this morning. The concrete of the offices has not been cleaned during holidays.

Jan 16th 1922 Douglas Stuckey has measles. Consequently he and Kenneth are excluded 3 weeks.

Jan 27th 1922 The contractor commenced work on the playground today - it is to be levelled, stoned, gravelled, tar sprayed in summer.

Jan 31 1922 Miss Kingcott away today ill. Miss Powell in charge of infants for the day.

Feb 20th 1922 Re-admitted K Stuckey. D Stuckey suffering abscesses in teeth. Admitted N.B. Latham visiting their grandfather Mr H Sweet for a week or two.

Mar 14th 1922 Miss McDougall visited the school this morning, recommends field be obtained for games.

Back Row 4th Mabel Traves **Row 5** 4th Cyril Wallis 5th Ken Stuckey
Row 4 2nd Jack Travis Row 3 7th Dennis Wallis
Headmaster Mr William Sheppard and Teacher Miss Kingcott
Revd. Green next to Mr Sheppard. **1920**

Back Row left Kate Ford Winnie Traves Margaret Powell
? Sweet Mr Sheppard Frank Stuckey Jack Kerton
2nd Row Mabel Traves P Sweet Beryl Young Diana Masters
Betty Masters
3rd Row J Sweet ? Ciss Scribbins Jim Powell D Sweet
Ruth Norton Olive Parsons
Front Row Percy Stuckey Doug Powell Cyril Wallis
Jack Palmer Dennis Wallis Ken Stuckey (Janet Burdge) **1920**

Copy of Report of H.M.I. Mr T Johnson on visit of 8 Mch 1922:
This is now a very satisfactory village school. The Headmaster has to teach some thirty five children in Stds I to VI with only the part time help of a Monitor, but by careful planning individual work and private study for the two higher classes, he continues to keep all the children usefully employed.

Careful record is kept of the progress of individual scholars and reports embodying the results of the term examinations are sent to the parents at the end of each term.

Except for some want of attention to phrasing in reading aloud, which is noticeable both in the infants and junior classes, all the work in Elementary subjects is very creditable. A special word of praise is due to the intelligent Arithmetic of the highest class, to the thoughtful association of Nature Study with composition & drawing, and to the infants' clever raffia weaving and other handiwork.

The managers are to be congratulated on the recent improvement of the school buildings & playground, which are now in excellent order.
M. R. Green Correspondent.

Mar 31st 1922 School year ends this day. Staff Mr J Sheppard C. Head. Miss Kingcott S. Av Atte for Yr Endg 1922 51.

Apr 3rd 1922 Snow falling heavily at 9 o'c, 6 infants, 12 others present, meeting abandoned, registers not marked. The afternoon meeting also abandoned as snow still falling heavily, only 4 attended.

May 5th 1922 Owing to injury to knee and resulting synovitis, I have not been able to carry on my duties in school. Mrs Sheppard (cert) has taken charge, since Monday.

May 19th 1922 Resumed work Monday but on doctor's advice I was obliged to give up again on Tuesday. The correspondent is in communication with county office for a Supply Teacher to commence next week.

May 23rd 1922 took up duties as Temporary Head. M R Hale.

May 29th 1922 Two children have today left the school owing to their father working in another village (Elsie Davies, Dennis Lauder). Attendance good. Have today examined needlework and given suggestions to the teacher. The heat is still very great, 78 degrees in the shade, but the schoolroom is lovely and cool to work in.

May 30th 1922   Have today commenced to teach Rudyard Kipling's song "Land of our Birth" set to music by J.B. Miles.

June 13th 1922   Re-opened school this morning. Resumed work, my leg having recovered sufficiently to allow me to do so.

July 10th 1922   I tendered my resignation this day, having been appointed Headmaster, Banwell Prm School. Under the Geddes committee recommendation, it has been decided to replace the Master by a Mistress on grounds of economy.

July 17th 1922   Excluded G & T Carpenter (chicken pox). Notified school MO 21 July.

July 31st 1922 Excluded J Sheppard C.P.
John was the Headmaster's own son.

Aug 3rd 1922 Closed school summer holidays 4 weeks.

Since closing School, I have been notified that I have been released from my engagement as from Aug 31. Consequently I shall not return to School as I commence duties at Banwell 1 Sep.
I should like to express my thanks to the Correspondent & Managers for the uniform kindness I (and my wife) have received at their hands & especially to Rev. M. R. Green, Correspt., for the many ways in which he has helped me during the ten years I have spent in this school.
Wm J. Sheppard.

Chapter 8
The 1920s

Sept 4th 1922   Ethel M Clarke (T.C. 06/805) Staff Supply Tch. Began duties as tempy head today.

Oct 12th 1922   *Visited   the School and found everything satisfactory, good discipline & order being kept, work progressing satisfactory under Mrs Clarke, as supply.*
M. R. Green   Correspondent.

Oct 16th 1922   The newly appointed Headmistress visited the school today. Miss Kingcott was obliged to return home as she was ill.

Oct 19th 1922   Miss Kingcott returned to duty today.
School closed at the end of the afternoon session for the October holiday. It will re-open on Oct 24th when the new Hd Mistress will begin her duty.

Miss Hole

Oct 24th 1922   Visited the school, Miss Hole commenced duties as Head Mistress today.
M. R. Green Correspondent.

Nov 3rd 1922   Mr Hayward S.A.O. called, another message was sent to the School Nurse about the children's heads.

1923

Jan 9th 1923   Reopened School this morning. Admitted Winifred Carpenter.

Jan 20th 1923   Olive Neath sent home owing to sickness.

Jan 25th 1923   Alice Glassenbury sent home owing to heavy cold & sickness.

Jan 30th 1923   Miss McDougall, Physical Training Inspectress, visited the school this morning.

Jan 31st 1923 Received certificate for Phyllis B. Found to be suffering from pneumonia.

Feb 8th 1923 *Owing to excessive wet, the Infants Mistress was obliged to return home, fearing pneumonia & not returned 12pm & still asent by afternoon. MR.Green Correspondent.*

Back Row left ?--- Mabel Traves Kay Webber
Front Row Jack Travis Ruth Norton GraceTravis ?---

The School in 1923

Mar 22nd 1923 The Head Mistress away on Doctor's orders for Operation, County notified.

Mar 26th 1923 I take charge of this school temporarily from this morning, Charles L Schofield.

Apr 9th 1923 School re-opened this morning I have admitted 4 new scholars, transferred 5 from the Infant room to std I and moved all the other scholars up one standard. I shall work the school as far as possible on the lines Miss Hole desires but shall leave the syllabus for her to settle. A record of all work done will be kept.

Apr 13th 1923 John Palmer and Dennis Wallis made full attendances during last school year. Mary Griffin never missed after joining the school after Easter.

Sadly John Palmer died during the Second World War, his ship was engaged in the hunting of the Bismark. The Psalm Board in the church has a brass plaque which reads:

Given in honour of John Palmer
who died of his wounds 31 May 1941
while serving on HMS Maori
"At the going down of the sun
and in the morning we will remember them"

Apr 23rd 1923 Miss Margaret Powell is absent this afternoon as she is to be confirmed at Yatton. On Thursday next the school will be closed by request, on the occasion of the marriage of the Duke of York.

Apr 27th 1923 Mr Schofield finished his duties on this day.

May 17th 1923 Miss McDougall called to know if a field had been obtained for the children's cricket.

May 29th 1923 Re-opened school after Whitsuntide holiday. Admitted Mervyn Williams.

June 4th 1923 Admitted Albert Carpenter. Jack Travis exempt as sister has chicken pox.

June 5th 1923 Kenneth Stuckey not in school as he has developed a rash.

June 6th 1923 Douglas Stuckey not in school as he has a rash.

July 13th 1923 Miss Margaret Powell finished her duties today having received permission from the Education Committee to commence her new work before the end of the month.

July 27th 1923   Miss Kingcott granted leave of absence this morning to take two children to see the occulist at Weston-Super-Mare.

Sept 10th 1923 Re-opened school this morning. Phyllis and Audrey Baker have complained a great deal about their eyes. Have written to county occulist to make an appointment for them.

Oct 11th 1923   Miss McDougall, Drill Inspectress, called this morning and took Std II-IV for games in the playing field. She suggested ordering footballs and 2 ropes from the County Committee.

Nov 8th 1923 Admitted Alfred Newman from East Harptree. Age 8¼ years. Does not know his letters and so unable to write any figures.

Nov 12th 1923   *Miss Murray commenced her duties as supplementary Teacher for Stds I and II.*
M. R. Green   Correspondent.

1924

Jan 8th 1924 Re-opened School. Ivy Lampert left. Admitted Megan Griffin.

Jan 19th 1924   Wrote to the county medical officer to ask the school nurse to pay this school a visit as I have had several complaints from the parents about the cleanliness of the children's heads.

Feb 15th 1924   10 children went to Yatton to see the School Dentist.

Mar 3rd 1924 Deep snow prevented the school being opened in the morning. Afternoon attendance very bad, so asked Headmistress to dismiss the scholars.
M. R. Green Correspondent.

Mar 20 1924 Sent Betty and Megan Griffin home as they had a number of spots on their necks, legs and faces which looked like chicken pox.

30th May 1924 Mrs Burge came to school and complained that her child had been struck on the head by the class teacher. This

statement was untrue and the child was reprimanded for telling untruths.

Sept 13th 1924 Found the bodies of several of the children in infant room in a verminous condition. The County Medical Officer was notified and stated that he would send the Health Visitor as soon as possible, but they were very busy, The School Nurse has not been to school for 6 months. She was notified last January that it was necessary for her to visit school. Her visits are not continued and may have some effect for a few days but it does not last long.

1925

Jan 6th 1925 Re-opened school, Diana Masters has left; Sydney Lampert is absent with influenza and Raymond Wilson with Diphtheria.

Feb 2nd 1925 Admitted William Neath,

Feb 11th 1925 Ivy Friar complained of a sore throat. Her tonsils were very enlarged and she was sent home. Miss Murray absent with Influenza.

Feb 19th 1925 I wrote to Mr Hayward on Feb 11th drawing his attention to the fact that Frank Travis had been absent from school for three weeks with no excuse. The child has now been absent another week and no steps have been taken in the matter. The child has only made 189 attendances out of a possible 367, he is delicate but a doctor's certificate is never obtained. Edwin and Cyril Parsons are also absent every week for a day or two and plead ill health but no notice has been taken of these absences. There are two children in the village over 5, Orchard and Windmill. I wrote and told Mr Hayward who so far as I know has not bothered to look them up. They have not come to school. I have drawn the correspondent's attention to these facts this morning.

Feb 23rd 1925 Mr Hayward called at the school on Friday morning and promised to call on Mr Travis. Frank has not come to school today but is playing in the farmyard every day.

Mar 10th 1925 Miss Murray took Phyllis and Audrey Baker to see the Oculist at Yatton. One child is nearly blind, her parents refused to allow her to wear glasses.

Mar 31st 1925 Miss Kingcott returned home on hearing of the death of her sister.

Apr 1st 1925 The Children were promoted to their new classes. There are 30 children in the top class, 12 in the second and seven in the infants. After Easter 5 or 7 new children will be admitted. Mrs Wood and Mrs Forbes visited the school today and addressed the children in The Prevention Of Cruelty To Animals.

Apr 21st Re-opened school (*after Easter*) admitted 7 new children. 1st class 21, 2nd class 13 + 1, 10 infants. 45.

May 11th 1925 Dr Wood visited the school and certified that Gratton and Mervyn Williams have Whooping Cough, Eula Masters has Whooping Cough. There were 19 children in school with bad coughs, these I sent home until Thursday morning. The cases were duly reported to Dr Melsome, Medical Officer of Health for the district.

May 14th 1925 *The correspondent communicated with the Medical Officer of Health (Dr Savage) who replied no necessity to close the school, but that the Head Teacher must exclude all doubtful cases which must be sent home immediately.*
M. R. Green, Correspondent
I called on Mrs Griffin (Donald) last evening and asked her to keep Elizabeth home until her cough is better. She was thoroughly rude and sent the child again today. I sent her home. She is the only parent who objected to the children being sent home.

May 22nd 1925 During the week ending May 22nd one Infants, 3 in Standard 1& 2 and 12 in III-VII children were present. The children received individual attention and in their spare time Miss Kingcott and Miss Murray made apparatus to illustrate lessons.
The Health Visitor visited some of the children on Friday.

June 9th 1925 Received message from Health Visitor to send A & H Simms and A Glassenbury home, D Stuckey away ill.

June 26th 1925 Miss Murray absent today.
Visited School this morning, found Assistant Mistress St I-II away. Sudden illness refuted and cannot quite understand it as yesterday in perfect health.
M. R. Green, Correspondent.

Sept 1st 1925 Herbert Eglington has left school during the holidays as he is over 14, and Henry Windmill has left the parish. Three children were admitted. Christopher Vowells, Alan Buscomb, Denis Clarke. There are now 57 children on the register.

Sept 7th 1925   Five   girls attended the cooking class at Yatton today. Olive Parsons is absent through Mother's illness and …'s mother refuses to allow her to attend.

Nov 11th 1925   Dr McCleod has ordered me to stay away from school as he certifies that I am suffering from arthritis.
Notice was sent to the County Education office today and supply teacher was applied for.

Nov 16th 1925 Mrs S E Clarke 'C' taking temporary duties.

Dec 14th 1925 Resumed duties today.

1926

Jan 4th 1926 Admitted Mildred Glassenbury and Francis Tuck.

Mar 17th Miss Murray has developed influenza.

Mar 26th 1926   Examination held for 5 places in the county. Starting at 9.50 am and continuing until 3.30 pm. The Managers were present the whole time – M. R. Green 9.30-10am, HW Price 10-10.45, Edgar Harris 11am-11.45, Tom Simmons 11.45 to 12.30, Edgar Griffin 1.30-2.30, M. R. Green 2.30-3.30.

Apr 19th 1926 Miss Murray returned to her duties today.

May 4th 1926   Visited the school and liked the replies, all satisfactory and work progressing favourably. Presented certificates, the headmistress Miss Hole presented two books for those who had kept regular attendance for twelve months viz Messrs Jas Powell and Nev Newman. Also work-box to the girl who had made the best progressing in 1925 - Catherine Palmer. M. R. Green Correspondent.

May 31st Admitted Clifford Evans, Leslie Neath and Frank Carpenter. Owing to the reduction of numbers in the school, Miss Kingcott and Miss Murray have this day received their notices and an uncertificated assistant is to be appointed to take Infants and Stds I &II.

1927

Mar 8th 1927   The free place Examination was held and the managers invigilated. Ten scholars sat for the examination.

May 16th 1927 Dr Weaver visited the school today to examine --'s head. He took some samples of hair and sent the child home again.

May 18 1927 Elizabeth Griffin has passed the first part of the Free Place Scholarship.

June 3rd 1927 I this day terminate my duties as Headmistress of this School, the new Headmistress commencing after the Whitsuntide holidays. I wish to thank the Correspondent the Rev. M. R. Green for his many kindnesses and the help he has given me during my very happy years in this school.
G M Hole

Mrs Brown

June 13th 1927 *Mrs Brown being appointed headmistress in place of Miss Hole, commenced her duties today at 9 am.*
M. R. Green, Correspondent
Re-opened school this (Monday) morning with 45 on registers, 41 present. ----- is still absent from ringworm.

June 15th 1927 Mrs Ruth Brown Reg. No. 19/26,344 W/2.
Seven children went to Yatton this morning for dental treatment. All returned before 12 o'clock.

June 17th 1927 Library books received today. Circulated this afternoon (Friday) 22 books were taken by the scholars. To be returned following Friday.

June 24th 1927 Two boys made 100% this week. 94% for the whole school. Heavy rains prevented children living at long distances from making full attendances – Mary Griffin absent in order to attend Oral examination at Sunnyhill School.

July 1st 1927 The last two days (Thursday and Friday) have been very wet. Owing to lack of dry accommodation outside in the playground, the children staying in school to dinner had to remain in schoolroom. During the dinner hour a tennis-ball was thrown by Bert Harris which broke a pane of glass.

July 13th 1927 29 Children were examined by Dr Cooke Herbert. ------ ----- was not present. Mrs ----- refused to come herself, although a special notice was sent to her by the Head Teacher. ------- has been absent for over one year.

July 14th 1927 Phyllis Tozer, of Phipps Bridge, has been sent to a holiday camp at Quantock Lodge, Nr Bridgwater where she will remain from July 14th to August 11th 1927. Attendance at this camp is an attendance under Act 44.1(g) of the Day School Code. Phyllis Tozer will therefore be marked present on such times as the school is opened during the period above mentioned.

July 21st The news of Mary Elizabeth Griffin's success in obtaining a Scholarship for Sunnyside School has arrived this afternoon. This - the first Scholarship gained at 'All Saints Church School' - has caused great excitement. The children are celebrating the event by a free choice of lessons: clay modelling, reading, drill and counter-marching.

Aug 30th 1927 *The school was re-opened on Aug 30th at 9 am, owing to illness of Mrs Brown, Miss Scourse has taken charge. M. R. Green, Correspondent.*

Sept 23rd 1927 Mervyn Griffin and Albert Carpenter attend the clinic at Clevedon to have their eyes tested.

Oct 3rd 1927 R Brown recommenced school duties. 100% present. First time this year no one absent.

Oct 12th 1927 The weather continuing so exceptionally fine, with bright sunshine, the children have out of doors as much as possible. Extra lessons in drill with marching etc. have been taken. Two games of football, and two paper chases have been allowed as Extras. The girls did their paper chase remarkably well. They were allowed half an hour for the 'run'. The boys being allowed to go further were allowed three quarters of an hour.

Nov 11th 1927 Armistice Day. Friday morning the whole school paraded after Assembly and marched up to the Triangle for the service held to commemorate the day. The rector gave the children a very inspiring address in the schoolroom. Every child wore a poppy. The two biggest boys carried the Laurel Wreath and laid it at the foot of the Memorial.
Miss Shield left school today. She has been transferred to Christ Church Sch Weston-S-M. No one has been appointed to fill her place here at present.
WS Birkett, Esq, County Inspector, paid a visit to the school this morning. 44 children were present. The attendance keeps remarkably good. Only one child being absent half a day in the upper school, and one child living at a great distance absent one day during the week.

Nov 14th 1927 Mrs Ida W Williams commenced duties here today as a supply teacher in Miss Shield's place. She is taking the Infants, Stds I and II and needlework.
Nov 21st 1927 Monday morning. It is so terribly dark in school this morning that it is difficult to work properly. The children are being dismissed at 12 o'clock sharp and afternoon school will commence at 1.15pm instead of 1.30. This will enable dismissal to be at 3.15 pm so that children that live at a long distance may reach their homes in daylight.

Dec 3rd 1927 Wireless music lessons given by Sir Walford Davis have been Broadcast in this school on Tuesday aftn. The first time Wireless music was heard by very many of these children was on November 29th 1927 when it was brought in from School house for music in the dinner hour. The loud speaker was a wonder unto many.

Dec 6th 1927 Colds are very prevalent. Several of the children are suffering from sore throats and troublesome coughs.
The coke fumes from one of the slow combustion stoves are very noticeable and most unhealthy. The windows are obliged to be kept open to give a change of air, which causes a great deal of draught, when the wind is east. The attendance is good on the whole.

Dec 14th 1927 Mrs Williams again absent today. A wire came at 10.15 to give reason for absence – rheumatism.

Dec 21st 1927 The First Annual 'Prize Day' was held in this school on Wednesday afternoon. A 1st and a 2nd prize was given to the two 'top' in each std. from 0-7 and a prize book to every child as a Christmas reward. Three of the school managers were present with Mr Price in the chair. Mrs Atlay handed out the books and Mrs Williams presided at the piano. School work, recitations, songs, drill etc. composed the programme.

1928

Jan 9th 1928 Monday. School reopened this morning, 40 children present. Miss Davis commenced duties for 'infant room'. She takes Infants Std I & II and needlework throughout.

Jan 30th 1928 History and Nature lessons are now taken on Mondays and Thursday afternoons from 2.30 to 3pm. The children of Stds III to IV inclusive, listen to the wireless lesson broadcast from London. Notes are written on the board and each child follows with a textbook. The lesson is afterwards re-capitulated with teacher's aid. Readers are used in connection with History, whilst Spelling, Composition and Drawing are also correlated. The first batch of compositions which were written by all the children were sent to the BBC Educational officers – Savoy Hill – on Monday afternoon Jan 30th 1928. The subject of these essays was 'Winter Sleepers' or 'Creatures which hibernate'.

Feb 1st 1928 The School bell has been re-hung after two or three years rest. It was rung for the first time for morning school on Tues Feb 1st by Ronald Lampert as senior boy and in the afternoon by Cassie Palmer as senior girl prefect.

Feb 2nd 1928 James Powell's name was called from BBC London as having sent in good composition on 'Winter Sleepers'. This is the first time for our school to score in this composition.

Feb 15th 1928 The Head Teacher (R Brown) has been absent from school duties since Wedy. last Feb 8th with an attack of pleurisy. The Rev. M. R. Green very kindly took the seniors all day Wedy, half Thursday, again all day Friday. On Monday the 13 inst he was laid up with a severe attack of Gout, so Miss E Davies managed the school alone. A supply teacher is due Thursday am.

On Monday the 13th inst. at 1.30 pm Miss Robertson, the Needlework Inspectress paid a visit to examine the Needlework. There are only 14 girls from Infts to VII. The girls are taken by the teacher Miss Davies who was appointed for this subject.

School caps in school colours, brown and green, are being knitted by each girl. Miss Robinson was pleased with shirt patching done by Cassie Palmer. Unfortunately, the Hd Teacher is still confined to bed, but Miss R very kindly came to see her after needlework inspection. Miss Robinson expressed regret, saying she wished there was more competent help for the Assistant Miss D. Tuesday the 14th inst a lady visited school and lectured to the children for an hour on 'Health' Cleaning of teeth.

Feb 17th 1928 Miss Davies has had to conduct School unaided this past week, as Head teacher is still under Dr Woods.

At the beginning of January term 1928 the School was divided into three groups to form three 'Houses'. Each house has a school colour green, brown or yellow, the members wearing coloured badges for distinction. Two boys and two girls are elected 'prefects' – good results.

Feb 25th 1928 A new stove with fresh air inlet, has been fixed in the place of the old one, and is a vast improvement. There is now no smell from escaping coke fumes, which means a far more healthy atmosphere.

Feb 27th 1928 *Mrs Brown returned to her duties today after having pleurisy – the county secretary being absolutely unable to send a supply: The school was carried by Miss Davies, who was not fully qualified.*

M. R. Green Correspondent.

Mar 2nd 1928 There will be no school this afternoon, as the children are being taken to Clevedon by 'chara' to the cinema for a lecture and Prize Giving in connection with RSPCA at 2.15 pm.

The First School Football Team 1923

Back:?..., Ken Stuckey Cyril Wallis Doug Powell
Percy Stuckey Jack Palmer
Front: Jim Powell Sid Lampert H Eglinton Jack Travis
Dennis Wallis

Back Row Bert Harris Mervyn Williams Gratton Williams Clifford Burdge
Jim Powell Bruce Harris Cyril Parsons Denzil Palmer
2ⁿᵈ Row ?— Edwin Parsons Don Lampert Mervyn Griffin Freda Simms ?---
Cassie Palmer ?--- Olive Neath Don Harris ? Stuckey Fred Burdge
3ʳᵈ Row ?--- Biddie Lampert Winifred Norton Kathleen Carver Iris Baker
Megan Griffin ?--- Iris Baker Iris Blake Leslie Neath ?-- Phil Harris
Front Row F Carpenter Walt Neath Bill Neath ?-- ?—Cecil Neath
Headmistress Mrs Brown 1928 (Joyce Harris collection)

Back Row Den Wallis Clifford Burdge Jim Powell Bert Harris Arthur Sims
Gratton Williams Bruce Harris ?--- Teacher
2nd Row Monitress Freda Sims May Towser Myra Baker Phyllis Burdge ?---
Iris Carver
3rd Row Mrs Brown Olive Neath Megan Griffin Iris Blake Kathleen Carver
Biddy Lampert Winnie Norton Iris Baker ?---?----
4th Row Doug Stuckey Mervyn Williams Don Harris Denzil Palmer Cecil Parsons
?--- Fred Burdge Arthur Glastenbury Edwin Parsons Frank Griffin Bill Slocombe
Front Row Don Lampert Ted Neath Bill Neath Lesley Neath Dog
Mildred Glastenbury Leslie Towser Sam Cox Jim Cox
Circa 1929

Mar 16th 1928   The free place scholarship Examination was held today.

The invigilating managers were Messrs Harris, Simmons, Griffin, Luff, Price and Bate.

May 9th 1928 Mr Moore HMI visited the school today from 9.45am to 1.45pm. *The 'mental' given by the Head to form 1 was considered 'too difficult', sums involving large numbers must not be given in written work. 'Method' of working, rather than 'neatness and accuracy' to be remembered. 'Free composition' throughout all classes to be increased, 'errors' to be re-written in 'sentences' instead of single words.*

The answering of forms III, IV, V (seniors) in general knowledge was admitted to be good. Also the lesson given by the Head to Upper Groups on Vulgar Fractions was 'quite satisfactory'. Discipline was good but boys' heavy feet in running and the general appearance of very poor boots, also the many children 'poor and dirty' was noted.

Notes of lessons to be more fully entered up by Miss Davies in Infant Room. Carpentry for boys desirable as handwork. Mr Moore recognised the need of another Assistant in order to cope with the work of so many varied Groups, but said the county would not grant an addition. 41 children on Registers. 39 present, of whom 29 were in Big Room, forms I to V inclusive. 9 in Infant room = Std II and 4 babies. Total 39.

This Inspection gives no encouragement for the Head who has worked under great difficulties for the three parts of the year she has been in charge of this school. Miss Davies has been here 4 months – January to May. 13 of these 'poor' children were given dinners (65 a week) all through six winter months. Many have received garments – underclothing, stockings, jerseys, knickers etc. one boy came to school last summer in pyjamas. Such 'poor and dirty' children are more difficult to teach and get 'results' from.

No word of praise, or appreciation to encourage the unseen labours, nor the large amount of good that has been done, was given.

May 11th 1928 The attendance has dropped this week owing to two cases of measles (Arthur and Mildred Glassenbury) and several odd days for children sick.

May 25th 1928 School closed this afternoon at 3.15 pm for this Whitsuntide Holiday to reopen on June 3rd. Empire Day was celebrated on Thursday 24th. Rev. M. R. Green addressed the children on the weaving of the Union Jack. After singing the Hymn 'O God our Help in Ages Past', the school sang 'Land of our birth we pledge to Thee', the school saluted the flag. A march as far as the War Memorial on the Triangle preceded Recreation – after which lessons on the Empire continued in various forms for the remainder of the day.

June 4th 1928 School re-opened this morning after Whit Week Holiday. Only 14 out of 40 on reg. were present. Measles are very prevalent throughout the village.

June 7th 1928 Only 12 children out of 41 on reg. came to school this am. A notice received from Dr Savage ordering the school to be closed from today, Thursday 7th to June 16th was duly to hand at 10am.

Two left = Gratton Williams & May Tozer. One Admit = Geoffrey Knapp.

June 18th 1928 School is closed for another week... one child Phyllis Burdge has been removed to Clevedon Hospital with throat trouble, after an attack of measles. Winnie Carpenter, a consumption child in Std III, has had a severe haemorrhage & is now very weak & ill also after an attack of measles.

June 24th 1928 Monday School re-opened this morning after being closed for two weeks. 27 children present out of 44.

June 29th 1928 Several of the children who have returned to school are far from well and seem 'throaty'. They sing flat, and out of tune, and show signs of fatigue very quickly... An application has been made by the Head Teacher for a Monitress...

July 6th 1928 All the boys & oldest girls have gone up to Farmer Stuckey's field to play cricket this afternoon. This is the first game they have had this season.
Note: This field presumably is the one at the top of Yew Tree Lane which was used also for the village sports in those days.

July 12th 1928 Fourteen children, 8 girls & 6 boys, arrived in school this afternoon at 2.30 pm sent from Walworth, London to Kingston Seymour for a fortnight's holiday.
They will attend school as visitors, not full time scholars.
July 13th 1928 This afternoon the whole school went up to the Cricket field to watch the Cricket match. The thermometer in classroom registered 72 degrees.
Note: The village cricket field was in Back Lane.

July 16th 1928 Miss Chittenden, Teacher of Country Dances and Morris Dancing, is staying at the School House with the Head Teacher for this week, and will give special demonstration lessons in these dances to the senior scholars.

July 24th 1928 All the Upper School with 14 visitors from London, numbering 45 children altogether, were taken by charabanc to Bristol Zoo. En route, all places of interest were pointed out to the children, and a halt made at the Cathedral. The University, the Royal Infirmary, Art Gallery, Museum & Suspension Bridge were particularly noted.

Mr and Mrs Palmer and their daughter Gladys. They were the school caretakers and he was also the sexton. They lived in Rectory Cottage.

July 30th 1928 Miss Davies is absent this morning. She went home to Aberdare on Friday last and returns today. 40 children in school. One Teacher alone.

Sept 3rd 1928 School re-opened this morning. Only one child was absent. The number on the roll has dropped from 44 to 38. Albert Harris, the top boy of the school has left for 'Sexeys'... Miss Evelyn Kent commenced duties today as Monitress.

Sept 4th 1928 Seven girls started cookery today. They are taken to Congresbury by motor-car, leaving Kingston Seymour at 9.5am.

Sept 14th 1928 At 2pm the whole school went by Charabanc to Clevedon (returned at 6.30pm) for a Geographical Expedition, lessons were given by the Hd Teacher to the seniors, & by Miss Davies to the Juniors & Infants to impress observations.

Oct 10th 1928 This being 'Health Week', extra time has been devoted to the subject of Hygiene in place of Nature Study & Drawing. On Friday morning Essays were written by senior scholars on the subject of 'Health'. Juniors had Sentence forming, dictation on the same subject.

Nov 2nd 1928 Miss Davies left the school today, she has been transferred to a Girls Dept. for Std I only at Pill.
Nov 12th 1928 Mrs Dorothy Marshall, Trained Certf Assistant Mistress, commenced duties here this morning.

As her experience has always been with senior children (Stds III and upwards) at Laira Green Girls School, Plymouth, Mrs Marshall is taking the work with the Seniors whilst Evelyn Kent takes the Babies in the Infant Room & Head Teacher is working with the Middle School children.

Nov 19th to 23rd 1928 Terminal Examinations are being held this week. On Friday Nov 16th, a heavy gale swept over the country, doing a great deal of damage everywhere. Many tiles & part of the Crest, were ripped off the School Roof. Trees crashed just outside the School, the noise of wind & falling tiles was very alarming. The children were sent home at 3.15pm.

Nov 26th 1928 The school is terribly draughty & cold. The Crest has not yet been replaced – a long open joint shows the sky & lets in a perpetual current of cold air. Our stove cannot be lighted, as the fumes & smoke from it are so objectionable. Teachers and many children are suffering from head colds & sore throats.

1929

Jan 21st 1929 Friday School re-opened this morning with 34 children present out of 38. Arthur Glassenbury left, & Grantley Carpenter admitted.
The weather is very cold – rhynes are frozen – snow falling. The Infant Room regr. only 30 degrees by thermometer. At 12 o'clock it was up to 45.

Feb 11th 1929 A very heavy fall of snow, with driving snow storm, has come this afternoon. Many children live at a distance, so school has closed at 2.45pm & children sent home.

Feb 12th 1929 Only 18 children are present this morning on account of inclement weather. The schoolrooms are terribly draughty & cold. The temperature in each room is down to 38 degrees. The children's hands are too cold to write properly, all have nasty coughs and colds. The attendance dropped to 14 scholars in the afternoon. Mrs Marshall was not present… Children sent home at 2.45pm. Head Teacher in charge, with temp 102. All present coughing badly.

Feb 18th 1929 Monday …The Head Teacher still had a temperature of 101, so instead of going into the draughty school room batches of children have come in turn, into the house sitting room. Lessons continued there…

Feb 22nd 1929 Miss Marshall absent today, on account of severe cold.

Feb 25th 1929 Miss Marshall still away – not returning to this school – gone to Pill.

Feb 26th 1929 Tuesday Mrs Edith Lewis from Merthyr commenced duty here today. She will be responsible for Needlework with the girls, take full charge of the infants, and supervise when possible Stds II &II. Evelyn Kent as Monitress will help in turn with the various groups. Snow again today, only 29 out of 35 children present.

4th Mar 1929 Head Teacher tried to commence school at 10 to 9am but was so weak and faint that she had to remain in the house, and take her classes in the sitting room. Miss Lewis managing nicely in school.

8th Mar 1929 Friday All the older scholars Std II to VII went at 2.30pm to attend 'Prize Giving', (Iris Carver, Douglas Stuckey, Mervyn Williams, having won a prize each for composition). 'Pictures' at the Clevedon Picture House. Mrs Lewis in charge. They are conveyed to and fro by charabanc – Mrs Vaudrey of Clevedon very kindly defrayed all expenses.

Apr 9th 1929 School re-opened today with 34 children present out of 38. Edith Kingcott, George Glassenbury were admitted.

Apr 16th 1929 The Hd T came in after end of aft'noon session yesterday with temperature of 103.5. Dr Wood was sent for and now orders bed for a week – on account of return of flu. A Dr's certf to that effect has been sent to county immediately. Rev. M. R. Green came and took scripture Tuesday morning and remained in school until 12 o'clock. Mrs Lewis and Evelyn Kent managing now alone.

Apr 18th 1929 Thursday, 14 boys have gone to see the Works at Swindon today *(this would have been the Great Western Railway Works);* Mr Wilfred Griffin, Scoutmaster, very kindly gone in charge. Olive Neath home with Scarletina, as Dr Wood was here to see me this morning, I asked him to look at Ted Neath's hands they were peeling. Dr pronounced Scarletina – immediately ordered all that family to go home. The five boys were dismissed – three with sore throats.

Apr 22nd 1929 Monday Miss Kathleen S Case from Walton St Mary, has been sent here by county council from Clevedon Council School to assist Mrs Lewis in school during the Hd Teacher's enforced absence; Miss Case is acting as a Supply Teacher at rate of salary £93 per an.

ETH Hawkins, Sanitary Inspector from Flax Bourton came to see about the fever cases this afternoon.

Apr 25th 1929 Dr Wood has ordered the Hd Teacher to go away for ten days to regain lost strength after long attack of Flu.

Apr 30th 1929 Dr Acusane, Thos. Hawkins Sanitary Inspector from Long Ashton, examined all the children owing to outbreaks of scarlet fever, thoroughly examining them, stating free of all infection – and ordered the school to be disinfected by spraying and scrubbed on Saturday.

May 2nd 1929 M. R. visited the school and stated that Mrs Brown will be away a further month owing to her illness and advice of Dr Doone of Illfracombe.

May 17th 1929 *Miss K terminates her engagement as temporary assistant – The school closing for the Whitsuntide Holidays. M. R. Green (Chairman)*

Sept 27th 1929 School re-opened with Miss LM Baker Reg.No 00/1938 in charge 33 scholars present.

Sept 30th 1929 Miss Baker finished her period in charge of the school.

Oct 1929 *visited school tested registers – Miss Gray commenced duties as supply.. R. Green (chairman)*

Oct 31st 1929 Mrs C Lewis terminated her engagement at this school today.

Nov 4th 1929 Miss Lily Hopper commenced duty here today. She will take charge of the infants.

1930

Jan 9th 1930 Six girls started cookery today. The class is at Congresbury, they go by motor leaving Kingston Seymour at 9.30 am. Miss Robinson visited the school this morning. Most of the girls were at cookery but she examined their work and reported it very poor.

Jan 14th 1930 Mr Snellgrove visited the school this morning to question the children with regard to the re-organisation of the school. He examined their written work.

Jan 17th 1930 The school to be closed on this day owing to the induction of the Rev. M. R. Green

(Bob Ford)

Note: The Reverend Major Revel Rayner Green was Curate-in-charge at Kingston from 1905 until 1930. He was appointed curate-in-charge after George Herbert Smyth Pigott, who had inherited the living, was prohibited from carrying out clerical duties. Rev. Green was ' presented' by the University of Oxford because the Smyth Pigott heir at Brockley Hall had become Roman Catholic. When the old Rector died and the curate at last succeeded to his rightful title, the bell-ringers marked the occasion by installing a tenor bell and dedicating it to him. The bell-ringing captain was W Scribbins (father of Charles). The other bell-ringers named on the plaque in the church are E Baker, W Griffin, J Kerton, E Norton, F Neath, AW Price, HA Price & A Price.

H. M. I. Mr report of April 3rd 1930:
This school has been very unfortunate since the last report of February of 1926 was written. The Head Teacher then in charge was appointed in June 1927 to a school in another part of the county. Her successor, who has not been teaching for many years,

has had very bad health and has been out of school since April 1929. She was unable to do justice to the children although she worked as hard as her physical disabilities would allow. During her absence the school has been in the charge of three supply teachers... It is much to be desired that the school should have the benefit of a settled and experienced staff. Adequate progress is impossible under present conditions.

School Memories from Megan Harris (Nee Griffin) of Mendip View Farm.

Megan was taught in the Infants by Miss Kingcott and remembers that in the large classroom, the floor was on two different levels by the window.
Rev. Green was often in the school taking assembly.
Later she was taught by Mrs Brown who was orderly and interesting, as well as the three Rs she taught a lot of geography. Sometimes the class would go into the teacher's home to see slides that were shown by Mr Brown. Although Mrs. Brown's health was fragile, she gave the children a rounded education.

School plays were always an event, The one that stands out for Megan was her wearing a Welsh costume and singing with Walter Neath who had such a good voice that he sang the top part while Megan sang the lower part to 'Where are you going to my pretty maid'. They received three encores!
At playtime the girls and boys had separate play yards. Her best friend was Biddy Lampert and they played the usual games of Hop Scotch, Ring-a-ring-a-roses and skipping.
At first Megan walked to school, back home for lunch, then walked back for the afternoon and home again at the end of the afternoon. Megan lived at Mendip View Farm. To break the length of the walk, she would walk between the 1st and 2nd telegraph poles, then run between the next two, repeating this alternately all the way. When she was older she rode her bike to school.
School was a happy time. She also remembers Miss Hole who left to go to Sunnyhill School, Bruton, where eventually Megan also went to school.

Chapter 9
Mrs Maslen

Sept 2nd 1930 School reopened - 30 on roll. Mrs A Maslen TC 17/1200 commenced duties as Head Mistress. Miss L Hopper absent (illness).

Sept 5th 1930 Miss L Hopper died.

Oct 10th 1930 No appointment yet made to fill vacancy caused by Miss Hopper's death, neither any supply. School therefore handicapped and work progressing under difficulties.

Oct 20th 1930 Miss Browning commenced duty here today as Temporary Assistant – School reorganised. Head Teacher being responsible for 3 Rs throughout the school, and Miss Browning being responsible for Geography, History and Drawing

1931

Feb 2nd 1931 Miss Buxton (certified) commenced duties.

July 1st 1931 Educational year begins. Promotions took place, School divided for general for general oral purposes into two groups...the junior group consisting of 10 children aged 7 – 9 and the seniors 12 children aged 10 – 13. There are 17 infants from 5 – 7.

Oct22nd 1931 Visited by Rev AN Holbrook Diocesan Scripture examiner:
My first experience of this school was a very happy one. I examined the children in two groups. The infants and Std I were I fear just a little shy. But in their answers and expression work there was evidence of careful teaching of the simple Bible Stories and the events of our blessed Lord... The upper group gave some really good answers, and the children evidently love their religious subjects... School as a whole 'Good'.

1932
May 5th 1932 Miss Lamb visited the school and talked to the children for an hour on 'Fresh Air'.

Dec 15th 1932 Report of HMI Mr AM Moore Inspection:

The Head Teacher appointed two years ago has effected a very great improvement in the general condition of this school which is very promising. The children are bright, take a keen interest in their work and take pains over all they do. The freedom with which the infants and juniors compose orally is most unusual and is an excellent foundation for subsequent work in English. The Infant Teacher is being carefully trained and is doing very useful work in a thoughtful way.

Dec 23rd 1932 School closed for Xmas Holidays. In the afternoon a party was substituted for ordinary routine.

1933

Jan 19th 1933 School reopened 37 children on roll... Dorothy Durbin reported suffering from Chicken Pox, on instructions of the MOH Dr Savage the other three members of her family excluded for three weeks.

Feb 6th 1933 Mr Bate (Correspondent) has today informed me of the decision of Dr Savage (MOH) to close the school until Feb 15th owing to chicken pox.

Mrs Maslen in the schoolhouse garden with Judy.

June 12th 1933 School reopened (after Whitsun) one new entrant 38 on roll. Visit of school Dentist, all children eligible for joining scheme (with the exception of two families) availed themselves of it (23 in all).

Extract from School Managers Minutes:
A dance held in Mr E Griffin's field. A Jumble Sale in
November. Hire of schoolroom 10/-.

Dec 4th 1933   Captain Fitzgerald (PT) visited the school this afternoon and watched and instructed the chrn.

Pool Farm: Past pupils play tennis.
Dennis Wallis Percy Stuckey Jack Travis Bert Price
Mary Munckton Enid Kemp Kay Webber Win Webber
(E Baker collection)

1934

Apr 20th 1934   School closed by permission of County Sec for refresher course at Bristol Univ. Miss Buxton attended.

June 22nd 1934   School closed for day, by permission of the managers, for children and parents to take part in an outing to Burnham-on-Sea.

July 13th 1934   Attendance 38% for week. Chrn continue to develop whooping cough. Chairman has written to Dr Savage suggesting closure.

July 16th 1934   Acting on instructions from Dr Savage Headmistress excluded owing to presence of Whooping Cough in School House. Miss Buxton carrying on with Infts (6) and mixed (9).

Oct 15th 1934 'Milk in Schools' Scheme inaugurated. (28 chrn participating).

Oct 24th 1934 No School in the afternoon on account of Funeral of Rev. M. R. Green (correspondent and chairman of the managers).
Note: The Rev. Green was 68 when he died in office. Previous to coming to Kingston in 1905, he had been curate at Chilcompton. He was a bachelor who enjoyed shooting and hunting and was often seen with his gun and dogs. The Rev. Green was a Church of England Schools Inspector and would cycle to Yatton Station taking his bike on to his destination. Even though he was not paid a great deal while curate, he was a generous man to his parishioners, parcels of food and bags of coal being given to needy folk. The Rev. Green successfully rebuilt a thriving church with a large congregation and choir. He was a good preacher and a prayerful man, there is a tale about the time he took a service at Kenn in a time of drought. He prayed for rain and got wet through when cycling home! Three years after the 'Sporting Parson' died the villagers brought electric light into the church as a memorial to him.
Information from Bob Ford.

Nov 29th 1934 School closed in accordance with King's wish for a holiday to mark to the occasion of the Wedding of HRH Duke of Kent and Princess Marina.

1935

Apr 1935 Visit from Revd Cottrell, newly appointed Chairman of Managers.

Bob Ford's memories of his childhood:
I was born in Kingston Seymour in 1930 at Laurel Farm, Middle Lane. Kingston was for my childhood years a very different village from the one we are familiar with today. There were less than fifty houses. Mains electricity came in 1936 and then only to a few homes; we went to bed with a candle. There was not a water main until 1946. Mains drainage came in 1974. Horses and carts or traps were more common than cars. During my boyhood years Kingston Seymour, like hundreds of other villages, was a farming community. Here was a way of life that had changed very little for many years. It was a way of life that was familiar to our Victorian grandparents and great grandparents.

There had been many changes in the wider outside world. When I was young, I knew a man who was born in the village seventy years before me; he died when I was fifteen. Old Brown came into this world not so long after the railway came to Yatton; in his younger days people still trod the footpaths of England. He knew the fields those paths crossed both in and around Kingston. He started work at the age of eight scaring crows in the fields, fields crossed by quite long distance paths. By the time Brown died, V2 rockets had exploded in London and the technology was in place to send a man to the moon.

Here life continued much as it had done for at least sixty years. There were twenty-six farmers in the village in the 1930s much the same as in 1881. The number of workers had dropped slightly. With very few exceptions everyone who lived in the village was employed in agriculture here in Kingston. Within the village we still had a school and shops; we had a carpenter, dressmaker and parson. This was the village I remember as a boy. Here was a way of which had changed little for generations. It is now gone forever and soon will be forgotten. Life was lived in a manner of which my children and grandchildren have no conception.

Our school, in common with many others, was Church of England Foundation. The rector was Chairman of the Board of Managers. When I was a junior we said our prayers and sang hymns at morning assembly. The rector spent time with us each Wednesday morning. He over a period took each phrase of the Lord's Prayer and talked about it in language we understood. He did the same with some Bible passages. We all processed to the church for services not only for major festivals but also on Ash Wednesday and Ascension Day.

We were, by and large, a healthy group of children. We were in and around the farmyards; in and out of cow houses, pig sties and dog kennels. During the long days of summer we roamed freely and drank thirstily from rhines. The water was clear and clean but very soft. Coughs and colds were rare and digestive infections unheard of. I, in common with many others, had little time off school through illness. There was little emphasis on hygiene. Every drop of water had to be carried to the house. We bathed once a week in front of the kitchen fire, rarely washed our hands before eating unless they were very dirty. We, I think, acquired a natural immunity to many things. These were Kingston children seen through the rose-tinted spectacles of memory.

There were health hazards. The only vaccine available was for Smallpox. It was not always administered, yet I never heard of a case. One case of Poliomyelitis occurred many years later. Impetigo was present in one family. Measles, Chickenpox and Mumps occurred regularly, Scarlet Fever and Diphtheria less frequently. Just before I started at school a girl of three died after contracting Measles. A little later a boy aged six died after Diphtheria. He had been ill all his short life. He spent much of his time on a bed under an open veranda. I and my sister visited him many times. Many years later I was told he had TB of the spine. He lies in the Churchyard a few yards from the tiny cottage where he was born. Thirty-one were buried in the Churchyard in the 1930s. Seven were children aged between ten hours and seven years. Of the remainder, fourteen were between sixty-seven and seventy-nine when they died. Two ladies reached ninety-five and ninety-eight.

When I started at the village school in 1935 most of the children attended there until they were fourteen when they started work, the boys on their fathers' or someone else's farm, the girls doing domestic work at home or nearby. A few went to Wake and Dean's furniture factory at Yatton or perhaps the boot factory at Clevedon. Within two years a grammar school opened in Weston-super-Mare and a senior school, or secondary modern, in Clevedon. Those who went to Weston travelled by train from Yatton, a coach was provided for those going to Clevedon.

At Kingston we assembled at 9.00am; lessons continued until 3.30pm with a dinner break from 12.00 to 1.30pm. There was a shed in the playground for those who had bicycles. Those who did not, walked to school. There were two children, a brother and sister five and six years old, who walked nearly two miles. Nearly everyone went home to dinner. Those who could not brought sandwiches.

For a while before I started, school had been talked about at home. When the big day came I was quite happy to set out on my own. I made my way up the lane and called at the shop to meet a lad a little older than myself who I already knew. I and a girl two months younger than myself were the only two starting that year. The infants' room with the passing of the years, seems to have shrunk. Then it seemed so big. There was a tiled coal-burning grate across one corner with a high fireguard around it. Nearby was a low table with six little chairs with wooden arms. These were for the six youngest. The older boys and girls had desks at the other end of the room. The letters of the alphabet were on the wall with a suitable illustration at the side of each. I do not remember how much I had learnt before school. I enjoyed lessons and soon knew my tables, liked sums and had become an avid reader. Singing seems to have played a big part in school proceedings.

Soon came an incident which became a lasting influence throughout my life. One morning my father, who had business in Clevedon, decided I needed a haircut. Either the business or the haircut took longer than expected. I was dropped at the school gate and a few minutes late dashed in. I was very soon made to know I had committed a most serious offence. I was taken through to the headmistress. I remember the serious expressions on both teachers' faces. What shall we do with him? I thought I was going to lose my head. To be fair, neither teacher offered physical violence. I was never late for school again and punctuality became a life-long obsession.

Mrs Maslen was a strict disciplinarian and a very good teacher. I know there are many who remember her with respect and affection... years later I received a letter from her son Peter Maslen. When they left Kingston they went to Sampford Arundell where Mrs Maslen was Headmistress, they then moved on to Henstridge where Mr Maslen was Headmaster and Mrs Maslen taught the infants. In 1955 they retired to near Wiveliscombe and later to Salcombe where they spent the rest of their lives.

Peter brought his mother back to Kingston when she was in her ninetieth year. They went down Ham Lane recalling Peter's school friends Mervyn Redman, Joyce Wallis, and Frank Kingcott. They tried to find Ham Lane Station where Peter caught the train to school. They looked at Middle Lane where 'Bill Travis kept pigs Danish style' and went along back lane past Enid Parsons' and Maurice Bagg's. They remembered them and many others, not forgetting 'The Rev. Green, that most splendid old reprobate and his suffering housekeeper Lily'.

1936

Jan 28th 1936 The school was closed with the committee circular – and the children attended a service in the church, it being the funeral of HM King George V.

Oct 1st 1936 Received 3 desks, a teacher's desk for infants room. This completes the refurnishing of the school begun in 1932 – it is now equipped with modern up-to-date furniture throughout.

Nov 11th 1936 Armistice Day. Children attended service and commemoration in church at 10.45am and afterwards went home until afternoon assembly.

1937

Jan 14th 1937 Head Teacher (Mrs Maslen) today gave notice to the Managers to terminate engagement here to expire on April 5th.

Feb 22nd 1937 Dr Newsome MOH called re diphtheria case - Harold Glassenbury and Cecil Neath excluded (suspected).

Feb 26th 1937 Dr Newsome called – the two boys referred to above returned to school.

Elsie Simpson who was Miss Buxton 1933 – 1938

I came to Kingston School after spending a year at Tickenham as a monitress. The vicar who interviewed me was the Rev. Green. He had been curate at Wrington so straight away he said he knew my Grandmother who lived on the Wrington road. Kingston school was a church school and I was a Methodist – not a good beginning, but he overlooked this. He knew all the children and he knew their families.

Mrs Maslen was the recently appointed headmistress. She had a break from teaching while Peter was very young and came back keen and full of enthusiasm to do things in the most up to date way. I was pretty inexperienced and was willing to follow her lead.

Her husband was a good handyman and made quite a few pieces of infant equipment painted in bright colours to look attractive. The two classrooms were freshly painted, and my class in the smaller room was small enough to be easily and happily handled.

There was a coal fire for winter heating with a big iron fireguard for safety.

The children had a 1/3 pint bottle of milk at mid – morning and straws were provided to drink it with. This was provided by Mr Dennis Wallis who delivered it in a crate each morning. Most of the children enjoyed it with a small snack from home. There were no school dinners, most of the children went home. The village consisted almost entirely of farming folk, either owners or labourers. There were no buses, the nearest station was at Yatton, a horse and cart was still part of the transport, and I had to cycle to get to school. It was quite a lonely road and I remember seeing real gypsy people camped in the lane off the road. The children begged for anything but did not come to school; the parents made and sold clothes pegs and lived in a covered wagon pulled by a poor looking horse.

The village children mostly came from secure homes where the parents were hard working. The boys wore heavy boots and were used to doing jobs on the farms. I remember Peter Maslen having sandals which he didn't want to wear because they made him 'different'. The little girls down the road had a pet lamb which followed them to the school gate. It was a very rural setting where children were encouraged to learn. They mostly read very well by the time they moved to the big room. They were taught by a method which was in the fashion at the time. It was called the sentence method and it produced good readers. Our books were all new, bright with pictures, and acceptable to small children. They were taught in small groups and helped each other. The inspector who came were quite impressed with the work we were doing.

We prepared for Xmas with enthusiasm making decorations for a Xmas party which was fun for us all.

I taught all the girls to knit and sew and we made some good garments by hand. I was once defeated by a left handed girl who never did quite learn to knit. I couldn't do it her way and she couldn't do it mine!

Eventually the day came when our number fell and I had to leave. There must have been a shortage of money for school even then, but I left with real regret.

Can you imagine a school now without television, computers, telephones, etc.? but our children were basically competent when they left us and they had a happy childhood without bullying or undue pressure.

Extract from School Managers Minutes 1ˢᵗ March 1937:
Mrs Maslen appointment terminated.
A letter from the Chief Education Officer with regard to
the Scheme of Re-organisation of Schools. ' In the scheme
Kingston Seymour was included in the group which goes to
Clevedon, where a new senior school has already been
provided. Mr Birkenshaw pointed out that the change of
head teacher presented a favourable opportunity for
dealing with this question & he suggested that we should
now arrange for the children over the age of eleven years
to be transferred to the Clevedon Council Senior School.
The Committee would convey the senior children to &
from Clevedon morning and afternoon. After discussion,
managers agreed'
Estimate of £4-4-0 nett for installing electric light in the
school.

Apr 6ᵗʰ 1937   Mrs AL Walker, Staff Supply Head Teacher in
charge of this school.

May 11ᵗʰ 1937 School closed to-day after the afternoon session for
the Coronation of Their Majesties George VI and Queen Elizabeth
which takes place tomorrow.

Back Jim Summerell Rosemary Fletcher Bert Parsons
Front Gladys Carpenter Tony Bailey Roy Wallis Dorothy Griffin
Marigold Ford

Chapter 10
Mrs Coghill and the Second World War

July 1st 1937 I come to this school as Head Teacher to-day. Muriel Coghill.

Memories of Ruth Jones

My very first memories are of being in the little classroom in front of the stove with a large guard and lots of heat and Miss Buxton rubbing my hands as they were so cold. Maurice Bagg took me to school, at midday he took me home and my mum gave us both cooked dinner – cold meat and veg. Marjorie, his sister, went to Auntie Gertie and her Gran's at Rustic Farm. We used to go down to school through the churchyard if we were late. It was a shortcut but Mrs Coghill told us we must *never* run in the Churchyard. It was disrespectful. She taught me most of my manners and morals. I was often sent to Mrs Coghill's house when I was nine to shake the mats and feed the grey & red parrot - he squawked a lot!

I often had to mind the little ones, I tried to teach one boy to read, never did, then Marjorie Bagg came in as a teacher's monitor.

Dad, as far as I know, at that time, was the only local farmer to have a license to sell milk retail to the villagers and school. Mum had a large white enamel pan into which she floated the milk in the boiler. She would bring it to a certain temperature and used a long thermometer about a foot long to test it. Each evening we put it into the bottles and then the cardboard caps were put on in the morning. All this with Mum's arthritis getting steadily worse. I had to cycle on my fairy cycle up to Yatton to Griffin's shop to order and then collect the bottle tops and the straws. I used to take the bottles of milk to school every morning in my doll's pram. Mrs Coghill used to stand the crates of milk beside the round coke-stove, it was horrible with the thick skin of clotted cream on top and being a bit warm. I had to keep a register of who had milk and take the money, ½ d a day each. I think the government topped up the payment for the milk to Dad.

Mrs Summerell came to us for milk, the boys would come with an enamel jug, the 8d a quart rattling in it. Mrs Carver also had 2 pints. I had to take it to old Miss Hale in one of Simmons' cottages, she always wore a rag around her neck. I also took it to Mrs Scribbins.

One day in the winter, going home at dinner-time, we were trying to break the ice in the ditch opposite the church edge of the Rectory garden. I used an empty milk bottle to reach across to the ice and then fell in, so I was then a true Kingstonite at 8 or 9 years old! Mum was *so* cross with me, I was soaking wet and stinking.

Mrs Coghill told us lots of stories about the Congo. We also had the Children's Corner in the church made when I was about 8, I was often sent over to clean it and polish the table and floor.

I was happy at school - and extra so when Mrs Fountain came as a teacher and taught me joined up writing. I was just 11 years old then.

I hope that you enjoy reading this, it was fun remembering.

Oct 8th 1937 This Morning from 11.5-11.25 for Juniors and from 11.25-11.45 for infants the Singing lessons was replaced by Music and Movement, as broadcast by Miss Ann Driver, in the programme for schools. This afternoon from 2-2.30 the children listened to a Travel talk on Guiana.

A local newspaper report highlighted in some detail the nativity play performed that Christmas for the first time.
A temporary stage was erected at the chancel steps in the church and 'with special lighting effects, the play was a colourful but solemn recital of the nativity of our Lord.'
Mrs Coghill and the Rector, Rev H A Cottrell were responsible for the production. Miss Enid Parsons 'brought a dignified presence to the character of the Blessed Virgin'. Mrs Baker was the Angel Gabriel and Miss Webber was the inn- keeper's wife.
The male parts were acted by Denzil Palmer (Joseph) while the shepherds were played by H Burston, J Baker and F Fletcher. Vera Norton was Zillah; the other shepherds' children being Margaret Harris, Bobbie Ford and Gus Fletcher. The angels were Violet, Joyce & Gladys Carpenter, Marigold Ford, Ruth Jones, Rosemary Fletcher and Vera, Edna & Dorothy Griffin.
'The cradle song was sung by Mrs Ford, and the introductory poem recited by Gordon Summerell. Mr J Stansfield was at the organ.'

Nativity play 1937 produced by Mrs Coghill.

Back Row Harold Bunstone Violet Carpenter Kay Baker Denzil Palmer Jack Baker
?--- Win Webber Frank Fletcher
Front Group (left of the Crib) Vera Griffin Gordon Summerell Edna Griffin
Vera Norton Gus Fletcher Dorothy Griffin Mari Ford Enid Parsons
Front Group (right of the crib) Rosemary Fletcher Bob Ford Gladys Carpenter
Ruth Jones Margaret Harris Joyce Carpenter

Angels
Violet Carpenter
Marigold Ford
Dorothy Griffin
Edna Griffin
Vera Griffin
Rosemary Fletcher
Gladys Carpenter
Joyce Carpenter
Ruth Jones

Angel Gabriel- K Baker
Joseph- Denzil Palmer
Mary- Enid Parsons

Inn Keeper's wife - Win Webber

Shepherds Children
David- Bob Ford
Elizabeth- Margaret Harris
Bartemeus- Gus Fletcher
Poem recited by Gordon Summerell

Children with Surprise Guest

1938
Back Row Left Margaret Harris Ruth Jones Mrs Coghill Jim
Summerell Bert Parsons
Front Row Gladys Carpenter Dorothy Griffin Sheep Rose
Fletcher Tony Bailey
Front Left ?--- **Front Right** Roy Wallis
(Edwin Parsons collection)

Marigold Ford remembers Kingston Seymour Village School:

I remember Father Christmas coming to the school bringing us all a present from his sack. It was Mr Coghill under the red, white trimmed gown and beard. While talking to us he told us he had left his sleigh in "Mrs Simmons Lane" beside the School House. I hoped to glimpse it afterwards, but by the time we went out to go home it had gone! My present from Santa was a book of *Snow White and the Seven Dwarfs*.

One fine summer we had a school play (or plays) on the Rectory lawn (the lawn to the left of the rambling old house). Ivor Kingcott was Knight or King and rode in front from the road clippity-clop on a real large brown horse. A troop of little soldiers had made their own wooden swords and my mother their red crepe paper hats. Jimmy Summerell's hat was our big leather-look tea cosy from home and it lasted years after that. One play was called 'The Green Imp'. I was the imp (still am?) skipping around the fairies singing "here comes the green imp, the GREEN imp, here comes the green imp to tease you all tonight". Then I was ordered to do tricks "Stand on your head, wriggle your legs" and so on which I did to our various mothers' amusement. My mother also made the fairies' rainbow, coloured crepe paper, gathered skirts, and matching frilled head dresses with knicker elastic to hold them in place. The crepe paper no doubt (as well as the elastic) being bought at Mrs Summerell's Triangle Stores. She was the kindest person of all remembered from childhood. All the little girls were thrilled to take their fragile outfits home afterwards.

One bitterly cold winter the rhynes were frozen solid and we children took great delight in walking right round the churchyard on the ice, well almost, apart from the few yards where Church Cottage (the home of the Carver family) then stood alongside the east gateway which remains.

A lady Doctor came to the school to give us our inoculations. As a small girl, I was afraid and had to be coaxed into the smaller school room where the Doctor was doing her awful deeds, by taking with me some drawings which we were doing to show her. At the first opportunity she jabbed me and I cried! I felt tricked, and have had a fear of injections ever since.

Library books appeared from somewhere. I remember taking home a book about other countries and it had music in it.

I learned 'O Christmas tree, O Christmas tree, how lovely are your branches'. It was only years later I realised the tune was that of the Russian National Anthem. As for the stallion being brought round the village he really was a lovely sight with his mane and tail plaited, and decorated with ribbon, but I didn't know then what he was for!

Mrs Coghill showed us collections of huge butterflies with six inch wing spans, pinned in flat glass cases that she and Mr Coghill had brought from abroad. She usually wore a dark dress with a white jabot on the front (a white bib-like removable decoration). One morning she had spilled boiled egg on it and I bravely told her about it and, as I guessed, she hadn't realised what had happened. She went around to her house at once and changed it. I am not sure how much she actually taught us, but a lovely summer afternoon would inspire her to take us, with Mr Coghill, on a 'nature walk' through the fields. The Reverend Gornall would appear in the school room unannounced (a school governor I believe). The chairs would grate on the wooden floor boards, as we all stood up. Also Mrs Voudrey, an elderly RSPCA lady from Clevedon, bless her, would come with the Inspector to talk to us.

There were stories too, rather tall ones, when we were children, of a secret passage from the sea bank possibly to the Rectory. The idea of pirates was fascinating as was that of a haunted room at the Rectory. Going home from school my brother Bob and I would look across from the road to the upper windows in the ivy covered walls, wondering which one it might be.

It all seems a long time ago, and it is, ten years more than half a century, and my few memories are only from the time of my own age group but it is lovely to look back and to know that from those early beginnings we all grew up happily and have made good of our lives. Who knows how much those early days influenced us? We shall never know.

Mrs Coghill wrote in my Autograph Book

'This above all, to thine own self be true
and it shall follow as the night the day
Thou canst not then be false to any man'
Shakespeare.

Back Row Margaret Harris Joyce Carpenter Gwen Carpenter Gus Fletcher
Ivor Kingcott Gordon Summerell
Front Row Ruth Jones Bob Ford Vera Norton Tom Simmons
Left of children Mr Joe Coghill   (Edwin Parsons collection)
1938

July 29th 1938   School closed until August 30th for Midsummer vacation. Miss Buxton left.

Gwen Carpenter

Extract from Managers Minutes 29th August 1938: Letter from County Education Committee informing Managers that owing to reduction of scholars in attendance, since the school became a Junior School, the services of the uncertified teacher must be dispensed with and a Monitress appointed in her place.

A requisition for school clock – resolution passed.

Aug 30th 1938   School re-opened. Miss Joan Wynn commenced duty as Monitress.

Edna Ridley (Griffin): Some memories of Kingston School and the War

I was brought up at Hope Farm. I remember having a pet lamb and we used to take it to the school playground sometimes, for the other children to see. I also remember the school milk being supplied by Mr Jones and also by Mr Wallis at one time. Strangely, because even though I came from a farm and was used to drinking it, I still really enjoyed the milk - this was probably because we got to drink it from a straw.

We often played rounders in one of the home paddocks of Mr Edgar Wallis (Cherry Tree Farm). I think it was the second field towards the back of the school, where houses are now. During the war, my father was an air raid warden and he had to stay overnight in the school, usually on a Friday. I saw the planes flying overhead when Bristol was bombed. My father took us outside in the night and we could see the sky, which was lit up absolutely bright red from the Bristol fires.

Another time, a sea-mine was dropped on the fields between Brittons Farm and Middle Lane Farm. It came down on a parachute, and blew out all the windows at the front of our house and the tiles off the barn. I went out there afterwards and picked up pieces of the parachute and bits from the bomb.

Isn't it funny, when I was a child the schoolroom was huge but when I've seen it more recently, it really seemed quite small.

1939

Jan 6th 1939 Clock for classroom arrived.

May 27th 1939 Miss Wynn (monitress) leaves today.

Mrs Joan Buxton nee Miss Wynn wrote to Joan Ridley in 2003, about her time as a monitress

As I was only 14 ½ years of age, I must say it was a bit strange at first but I soon became used to my little infant class who were always very happy children and quite willing to learn.
One thing that remained in my mind was taking the children to see the lovely Easter Garden which had been made in the Church.
I remember Mrs Coghill and her husband and they were always very kind to me. The Rev Gornall and his wife were very well liked when they came in to the school and lived opposite in a lovely rectory. I have lots of names going in my mind, Marigold Ford, Tony Bailey, Vera, Edna and Dorothy Griffin (Dorothy in my infants class). Ivor Kingcott, older class, also Edwin Parsons who lived in the first Brick House, Young Jimmy Summerell in my class. Nortons, Wallis, Harris, Griffins, Stuckey and Summerells at the corner shop.
I remember Gwen Carpenter with her specs, she lived with her mother in the cottage with the walk over the rhine back from the road.
I used to cycle to the school in the morning and cycle back to the Henly Lane, Yatton, for dinner then go back again for the afternoon school.
I had a good knowledge of the farms and names, my Dad knew of them, as he had a van selling most things on his round in those days.

Extract from Managers' Minutes 30th June 1939:
Mrs Coghill told the meeting that there was little or no need of the scheme at the school, and delivery of milk a difficulty.
Mrs Coghill acquainted the managers with a point of law about church schools viz. 'that a Church school could not be closed if the Managers subscribed at least 2/6d a year to the Finances of the school'. Agreed to do this. County Examinations awarded to Vera Norton, Margaret Harris.

July 3rd 1939 Miss Mary Pearce commenced duty as monitress today.

July 14th 1939 Miss Orr, County P.E. Organiser, inspected and expressed satisfaction with alertness of the children. She suggested the removal of a fence in the playground, which would give more space for physical training.

Aug 30th 1939 Pamela Usher admitted and staying here owing to the uncertainty as to her safety in London should war break out.

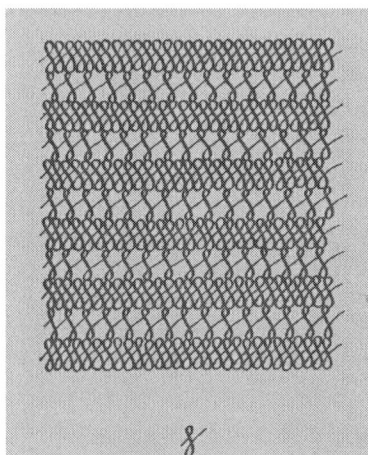

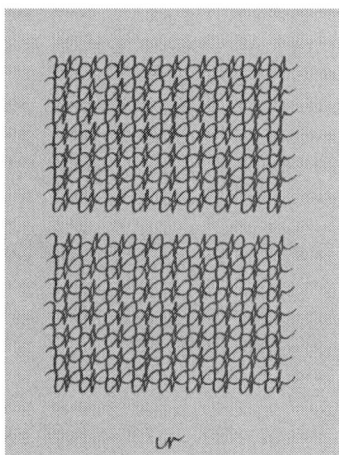

Handwriting taught from *Writing and Writing Patterns* by Marion Richardson.

Sept 1st 1939   In accordance with a Memorandum issued by the Chief Education Officer, the school was closed until further notice, pending completion of billeting arrangements for London Children to be evacuated.
The children were dismissed at 10 am after a demonstration on the handling and wearing of gas masks given by Mr Coghill, Air Raid Warden.

Sept 12th 1939   School was re-opened this morning. Five of the children evacuated from London were admitted, and their attendances entered on a separate register

Nov 17th 1939 Av Att. 28 = 95%
Henry and Reginald Law left this school today to return to London.

> *Extract from Manager Minutes 26th April 1940:*
> *...Managers reminded of subscriptions due May 15th of 2/6*
> *to ensure the maintainence of a school in this parish.*

June 14th 1940 An Air Raid Practice was held this morning and the children quietly took their allotted places in perfect order, within 3 minutes of the warning being given. Av Att 28 = 95%

The School at Kingston Seymour – Gus Fletcher

When I arrived in Kingston from the village where I had previously been living (Wellow, near Bath) it must have been in the year 1936, I think; I was about 6 years old. I had the inestimable benefit, in my Infant school in Wellow, of a wonderful teacher called Miss Parsons who had that happy gift of imparting knowledge apparently effortlessly and I was already a precocious bibliophile!

With more than my fair share of good luck I found myself in Kingston school with an equally splendid teacher (indeed teachers), for there was Mrs Maslen when I first arrived, to be followed by Mrs Coghill. I owe a great deal to both, but because I was inflicted upon Mrs Coghill for much longer, particularly the latter. Mrs Coghill 'pushed' books at me at every opportunity; Richmal Compton's 'William' books, those of J.M.Ballantyne, R.L. Stevenson – and many others. Some of these came from Mrs C herself, but there was in addition, I seem to remember, a regular (weekly?) travelling library when books arrived at the school in wooden boxes with rope handles; a cause of great excitement to the bookworms amongst us.

Mr and Mrs Coghill lived in the Head teacher's house at one end of the school. I think Mr C came from the Belgian Congo or somewhere in Africa; it varied in our fascinated discussions about this from Pigmy land to the equally exotic, and unimaginably remote, Ivory Coast. Not only that, but even more arcane, Mr C was said to have contracted the dreaded (we always prefaced the disease with 'dreaded' having heard it thus described by someone or other) 'Blackwater Fever', a matter of endless speculation as to how you got it and what the effects were (some of these, in our surmises were lurid in the extreme!) They had, again a matter of enormous fascination, certainly to me, a parrot which was, Mr C told us, an 'African Grey'. The bird lived in a large domed cage and was always climbing up the bars by holding on its beak. This was completely crossed over upon itself as a result of these avian gymnastics, as we thought, although in later life I discovered that all such creatures, even in the wild, had similar beaks!

I seem to remember that the school had a bell and that if one was allowed to ring it, it provided great cachet! A boy called John Eglinton, being a strong lad for his age got to do this more often than was fair, we thought! The school, which to small children, including me, looked huge, was divided into the 'little ones' and the 'big children' as far as I remember, and we enjoyed the attention of a junior teacher, in addition to Mrs C. Or was she, I think it was a girl, called a 'monitor? Lessons were taken very seriously, for although school leaving was at 14, I think, (from Kingston pupils went to the new 'Secondary Modern in Clevedon when they were 11 years old) there was the shimmering prize of 'the scholarship' awaiting us when we reached the magic age of 11.

Lessons apart, we seemed always to be busy with various school projects. There were 'Nature Walks', class singing, school plays, and, a major undertaking, a Nativity Play. This was cause for great effort on the part of just about everyone. I remember helping to cut out innumerable white crepe paper feathers, which were then glued to the wings, which had to be cut from sheets of cardboard, the ever-present 'Gloy' being brought to bear for this purpose. Gloy came in a pot with its own brush incorporated in the lid, and had the wonderful propensity of transferring itself onto hands, sleeves, and, with the minimum effort, even hair, much to parents' disgust when we got home. But we were proud of the end result, and the wings, when fixed with a harness to little girl angels, and with the addition of gold-painted halos made them look very holy indeed. The play took place in the church behind the school and photographs exist of this. I think it must have been staged in 1937 or 1938, but I can't be sure of this. I was 'Blind Bartimeus', my younger sister Rosemary was an angel, and my elder brother Frank a shepherd, complete with a long and rather Father Christmas-like white beard. Also at Christmas there were seemingly endless paper chains to be made for the classrooms and I can taste the gum from them (they had to be licked to make a loop) to this day.

Then there were functions in which the school played a prominent part such as bring and buy sales, fancy dress parades and, most exciting of all, 'fairs', and I recall most clearly the bran tub where for a penny you could make a 'lucky dip'. Odd how quirky one's memory is; I was standing at the tub, envious of those who were paying their pennies and winning the most wonderful treasures and hoping against hope that no-one would get the cap-pistol which I knew was in there, when a young mother came in to the school carrying a small baby, and groped in her handbag for a penny. Because of the infant she did this 'blind' and as a result dropped into the box a florin by mistake. This was potentially pretty ruinous for her, but the bran-tub operator saw the mistake and the two-shilling piece was replaced by a penny.

The school playground ran from the front of the school and round one side and seemed prairie-like in acreage (it has shrunk wonderfully over the years and when I saw it recently I wondered how we had all managed to run about in it without colliding with others at almost every step!). There was, too, a tree down in the corner near the road which we were forbidden to climb, and which, naturally, therefore presented us with an irresistible challenge to do just that.

Other disconnected vignettes come to mind; the large brown bottles of ink standing on the sill under the tall windows, the long poles with brass hooks on the end for opening the windows. The squeak of chalk on blackboard, a boy who bit his nails so badly they had to painted with bitter aloes (he got to like the taste so in desperation was put into cotton gloves which he duly gnawed through, at which point defeat was tacitly conceded). A new, very 'with it' school songbook arrived called, perhaps, something like 'The Modern Student's Song Book'. Not very popular, as I remember and we were aghast to be made to sing 'On the grassy banks, lambkins at their pranks, woolly sisters, woolly brothers, jumping off their feet, while their woo-oolly mothers, stand by them and bleat'. Not completely inspiring stuff for children who were surrounded by these animals although perhaps just about right for those children from the cities (some of whom we were shortly to meet in the shape of evacuees.) Much better were the works of Lear and I remember a boy, first name Gordon, declaiming 'The Owl and the Pussycat' to great applause. Church played its part in school life, nativity plays apart, and we all went off in crocodile for Easter, Ascension Day, Whitsunday and the other great festivals. Then there was Oak-apple Day which celebrated King Charles hiding in an oak tree. We all shouted 'Oak-apple day, oak-apple day, if you don't give us a holiday we'll all run away'. Did we get the day off? I don't remember.

I remember the sombre news of the dying King George V and the subsequent celebrations over the coronation of his son, George VI. The school organised a Sports Day on the field just over the lane from the Griffin's farm. I believe I may have won the sack race – but I'm bound to say that this might be wishful thinking.

The school, the church - there was also a chapel to which many of us went cheerfully, for they had all sorts of jolly hymns, particularly 'Sankey's Songs and Solos' and the preacher was a nice little man known to all, perhaps irreverently, as 'Hopper' because of a game leg, who made it fun, dividing us into 'crows' (boys) and 'nightingales' (girls) when it came to singing alternate verses - the seasons, haymaking, harvest festivals, Christmas, all were woven into the fabric of the village, but of all these I think the school played a pivotal role for not only did many of the villagers have children in the school but a great number of parents had themselves been pupils there.

June 26th 1940   By permission of the Managers, the school adjourned at 3pm to the Rectory Lawn, where they performed a play in aid of the Red Cross.

July 26th 1940   Air Raid warning at 1.40 am. Children remained under cover until 2.25pm when the 'All Clear' came through. Mr Hayward, the retiring Attendance Officer, called to introduce his successor Mr Bray.

Extract from Managers Minutes 30th July 1940:

Scholarship awarded to the school (Augustus Fletcher). Mr E Griffin referred to the probable use of the schoolroom (small) by the A.R.P. wardens at night – with the introduction of a telephone extension for the School House.

The Managers then inspected the small classroom to see the work done (by the L.E.A.) to protect the children for air raids.

July 31st 1940 School began at 9.30 am this morning and some children arrived later. This was due to the fact that everyone in the village had been greatly disturbed during the night, when enemy bombs were dropped in fields. Fortunately no damage was done.

Extract from emergency Managers Meeting Minutes 23rd August 1940:

Damage by Air Raid Aug 5th – 9th and repairs prior to the school opening.

Restriction of light by sand bags and cellophane strips to the windows and 'First Aid' blocking in of broken windows (22), rendered both large and small rooms gloomy for the children. The use of the smaller room had the advantage of needing no repairs to glass windows. Considered unsuitable by Managers because two teachers would have to work side by side and also because A.R.P. wardens would be using the room nightly until 5am. Managers ready to repair large room but another air raid would undo the work and expenses incurred would be lost. Agreed to submit dilemma to the Chief Education Officer and ask whether the smaller room would satisfy requirements while the war lasted.

Sept 9th 1940 School re-opened this morning, a week later than the prescribed date owing to the fact that repairs to the school, necessitated by enemy action, were not completed until September.

Sept 7th Miss M Bagg began duties as monitress. An Air Raid warning was given at 11.20 am but reading was continued in the Refuge Room.

Sept 11th 1940 Air Raid warning at 11.30am. Children remained in Refuge Room until 12 o'clock when the All Clear was sounded.

Sept 12th 1940 Air Raid warnings at 9.30am and 2pm.

26th June 1940 play on Rectory Lawn
Back Row Jim Summerell Harold Parsons Ray Stuckey Ken Clark
Front Row John Clark Cecil Norton Alan Summerell David Kingcott
(Cecil Norton)

The Ruston family at Rose Cottage
Stella Evelyn Maisie Betty Jimmy (Jim Ruston)

Sept 18th 1940 Air raid warnings twice yesterday and three times today. Work is continued as far as possible in the Refuge Room, but the constant interruptions interfere seriously with planned work.

Nov 27th 1940   Air Raid warning from 12.15 – 1 pm. In consequence the afternoon session began at 2pm.

Nov 29th 1940   Air Raid warning from 12.15 – 1pm. Afternoon session began at 1.50pm. Av att 33 = 94%

Recollections of Kingston Seymour School 1940 – 1944 by Jim Ruston

We arrived at Kingston Seymour in early October 1940 having been evacuated from London's East End during the Blitz. Mrs Kingcott who lived in the village with her husband and sons at Ham Farm collected us from Yatton Station in her small Austin car. There were six of us - Mum (Liz), May, Stella, Evelyn, Betty and me – Jimmy. A cottage had been found in order that we could stay together, very fortunate indeed considering the difficulties encountered by billeting officers at that time. Rose Cottage was owned by the Griffin family who farmed nearby at Mendip View Farm. It was about a half mile from the village where the junior school was situated. The school catered for children from 5 – 11 years, after which they went on to Clevedon Senior School 4 miles away. A coach was laid on to take children there.

Mum was naturally anxious to get her children to school as soon as was practical. May, Stella and Evelyn were of school age whereas me and Betty were not. But at least three of us would be off her hands during weekdays or so she had hoped. You can imagine my mother's astonishment when told that unfortunately Kingston Seymour School was closed, until further notice. The reason given was that an unexploded bomb was in close proximity to the school and not until a bomb disposal squad could be spared to come and diffuse it could the school re-open! We thought we had got away from the danger of the Blitz only to find a live bomb lurking just up the road!

After complaints made by the head teacher to the authorities the bomb was defused and on the 14th October 1940 May, Stella and Evelyn were enrolled. Although I wouldn't be of an age until my 5th birthday which was 17th May, my ever resourceful mother merely told a fib about my date of birth to get me in school at Easter instead of having to wait until the start of the winter term. "If anyone asks, tell them you're five," Mum instructed me. In fact one of my first recollections of the school was before I started there. To supplement her meagre income Mum took the job as school cleaner, she also cleaned the schoolhouse and the Rectory. Mum used to take Betty and I with her on her jobs. We walked from Rose Cottage, Mum pushing the pram with Betty in and me dragging along behind moaning. It was fine in summer but terribly bleak during winter.

In 1940 the headmistress was Mrs Coghill. Strict but fair, my sisters got along quite well with her. My teacher was Mrs Fountain whom I adored. This lady was dedicated to the children and demonstrated this by walking from Yatton to Kingston Seymour and back daily in all weathers. One winter my teacher got so wet, so often, she ended up with pneumonia – a very serious illness in those days.

I can remember quite vividly the Christmas school plays, they were splendid. One in particular stands out in my memory. Stella and Evelyn were dressed as trees and behind them children dressed as elves poked their heads round the 'trees'. All was going fine except that Evelyn's lisle stockings, quite obviously loaned by some kindly adult and too big by a country mile, kept falling around her ankles. She was far from amused. I had to join with others from the Infants and sing 'ring-a-ring-a-roses'. Reluctant that is until 'encouraged' by Mum to 'get on with it' – arguing with Mum was not an option.

Before my eldest sister May left the school to go to Clevedon, she took part in a writing competition. Several schools were involved and the results were published in the Bristol papers. You can imagine our delight when May won a prize for her essay. Some books, a framed picture of Jesus, and a postal order for seven shillings and sixpence were her reward. Quite a lot for a child in those days.

We attended school in all weathers. On occasions when Mrs Coghill, despite her very best efforts, was unable to get sufficient coal to keep a fire burning, reluctantly she had to declare the school would have to close. I can say with all honesty, and my sisters will back me up, I cannot remember being pleased when school closed for any reason. I loved it there, we all did. The teachers that looked after us during those dark and dangerous years deserved a medal for what they did. At times they must have had a heavy heart.

Kingston Seymour and its school has a very special place, not just in my memory, but also in my heart, a piece of which will forever remain there.

In the year 2000 I released my autobiography *A Cockney Kid in Green Wellies,* published by JR Marketing, on which I had been working for almost a decade. In it there is a chapter devoted to Kingston Seymour.

Dec 13th 1940   The Medical Inspection took place this morning, when Dr Cuthbert examined all the evacuees, in addition to those who were due routine examinations. She recommended that a cover be provided be provided for the cesspool in the playground.

1941

Jan 6th 1941   School re-opened this morning with 35 on Roll. Some children very tired, as a result of the noise on Saturday night, when 18 high explosive bombs and numerous incendiaries, were dropped in the village.

Jan 17th 1941   Attendance is low owing to illness among the children and last night was very disturbed owing to enemy action, many of the younger children are absent today, while those who are present, very tired.

Jan 30th 1941   No fuel available so school was closed.

Feb 20th 1941   Mr Kegan an inspector from the LCC (London County Council) called this morning to see LCC evacuee pupils he said that the LCC would provide financially for an additional teacher if the County Council would find one, as it is difficult to obtain a teacher from London…

Mar 7th 1941   The County Examination for Special Places in Secondary Schools was held today. Two Air Raid warnings were received in the afternoon but the examination was not interrupted as it took place in the classroom which is normally used as a Refuge Room.

Extract from Managers Minutes 10th March 1941:
The children had been medically examined. The report was
good, later most of the children had with parents' ready
consent been inoculated against Diphtheria. The number
of children on books was 39 and 41 was expected to be the
number after Easter.

Mar 17th 1941   Attendance bad this morning owing to a very disturbed night. Barrage fire continued until 4.00am.

May 8th 1941   HMI Miss Grant called at 10am and remained for half an hour noting number of evacuees present, number on roll, inspecting Refuge Room and finding it now very unsuitable for infants. She remarked on the unusual 'naturalness' of the children, who had been telling her of their part in painting the Hiawatha Frieze.

May 12th 1941   Mrs DM Wooster an LCC Infant Teacher took up duty this morning. The Assistant to the County Sanitary Inspector visited school today and suggested improvement in the sanitation. He also remarked on the danger of a bad atmosphere in the small classroom due to the use of same as a Wardens' Post at night.

May 23rd 1941   As Empire Day falls on Saturday this year, today has been chosen as the official date for celebrations in schools. Pupils and Staff have joined in making a collection for games equipment for the RAF contingent stationed locally. The Rector attended at 2.45pm and Robert Ford, one of the boys who had been foremost in organising the scheme, made the presentation to Sergeant Strange RAF.

June 3rd 1941   At 9.30 am only 10 children were present out of 44 on the books. The Head Teacher telephoned to the County Hall and was instructed to communicate with the Police Authorities in order to find out whether the presence of an unexploded bomb near the centre of the village rendered it dangerous to keep school open.
The decision of the Police was that it was definitely dangerous so school was closed until the bomb either explodes or is removed.

June 21st 1941   The Head Teacher, distressed at the prolonged closure, today telephoned the Superintendent of Police at Long Ashton, asking whether it would now be safe to re-open school. Superintendent Gregory said that he would reply after consultation with the officer commanding the Bomb Disposal Squad. He telephoned on June 22nd refusing permission to re-open the school on the ground that 'it is a legal offence to assemble children within half a mile of the unexploded bomb. To open school would render both the Education Authority and the School Managers liable to prosecution.'

July 16th 1941 The school was re-opened this morning as the G–mine was removed, fortunately intact, last night.

> *Extract from Managers Minutes 6th August 1941:*
> *The small room had been used to cope with the influx of Evacuees' children. The LCC had sent a teacher Mrs Worster (fr Limehouse)... LEA had asked the Managers to stack all the fuel they possibly could. Report from the County School Medical Officer dealt with the sanitary arrangements for the school children and the drinking water from the School Well being unfit for consumption. Sanitary arrangements, it was agreed that the influx of Evacuees had a deleterious effect & that Mr Bailey be asked to fix pails to the underside of the seats. Mr Palmer asked to see that these and the replacing of peat in the boys department be attended to as often as necessary.... A bucket for easy removal from the cesspit should be provided – to be supplied the same as the closets.*
> *With regard to the drinking water supply. Mr T Simmons said he would gladly let the children have all the drinking water they wanted – daily if need be. It was proposed & agreed that a white enamel bucket be purchased for this purpose.* (Note: Mr T Simmons lived at Court House).

Sept 17th 1941 Miss Rooke, County Dentist, inspected 25 children at Triangle Farm, the inspection will be continued tomorrow.

Oct 3rd 1941 School closes at the end of the afternoon session until Oct 13th so that the children can assist farmers with harvesting and potato-picking.

Oct 13th 1941 Mrs DM Fountain, certified Assistant, who came in place of Mrs Worster, took charge of the school when it re-opened today as the Head Teacher is absent on sick leave.

Nov 3rd 1941 The Head Teacher returned from sick leave today. As Mrs Fountain is experienced in teaching Juniors rather than infants she is continuing in charge of them, while the Head Teacher takes the infants.

Dec 12th 1941   After this week school will open at 9.30 am and close at 12.30 and open at 2.00pm and close at 4.00pm to provide a longer dinner break for children who live at a distance.

1942

Jan 26th 1942 Mrs Fountain returned to duty looking very ill. She finds the daily walk from and to Yatton station (two miles each way) very difficult in the inclement weather.

Feb 27th 1942 1 stirrup pump received for use in school.

Mar 9th 1942   New Attendance Registers and a new Summary Register were received today, also a parcel of rug wool, weaving wool, canvas and other handwork materials from Dryad Ltd.

Mar 16th 1942 Warships Week opened in the village. A target of £20 had been set for School Savings for the week but this was raised to £40 as School Savings for the week amounted to £114-5-0, a remarkably high total. £3-3-0 of this amount was released by means of a school concert given from 3.00-4.00 pm yesterday. Schoolwork has been terribly upset during this week. School has been used nightly for social functions.

Apr 15th 1942 Received 1 ton of coal, ½ ton of coke. Dr Cuthbert inspected the 22 children who were present, and also three who had mumps.
Miss Grant H.M.I. called to collect a Reading Sheet which she wished to use as an illustration for some lectures. Mr Bray, School Attendance Officer, called this afternoon. Form M.D.1 sent to local M.O.H. notifying eight cases of mumps.

May 14th 1942 Registers were marked at 8.55am. the children went to church as it was Ascension Day. They returned to school, drank their milk, helped with the salvage effort, and were dismissed at 11am for the rest of the day.

Extract from Managers Minutes19th May 1942   The suggested sanitary arrangements – the emptying frequently and a suitable place for disposal presented a difficulty. The number of Evacuee's children had decreased considerably – the problem was not so intense as a year ago. The Caretaker's husband, Mr Palmer said he used his own garden for the dump. It was resolved to see if a truck to assist the operation could be bought for the Caretaker. Caretaker's wages increased from £12 – 15 a year.

The matter of sanitation of the School House was considered & it was decided to ask Mr Bailey to report on the best thing to do.
Mrs Fountain appointed as a certified teacher at £240 plus 6% war bonus.
Circulars: E428 Re Women in Educational Service, Salvage, Protecting buildings, Young Farmers clubs, Easter Holidays.
E 422 Position of schools in Event of Invasion.

June 5th 1942 Miss Grant, HMI called this afternoon. She saw a country dance performed by the Juniors and Infants and was very pleased with the happy tone of the school.

June 30th 1942 No. of Evacuees on Roll = 11.   No. of Somerset children = 22.

Sept 29th 1942 Miss Anderson, School Meals organiser, asked to see the Head Teacher about the service of the hot meals at this school. It is hoped to begin this service in three weeks time. The meals will be sent from Churchill.

Oct 1st 1942 The Head Teacher has to go to Clevedon this afternoon to cash the salaries cheque. Mrs Fountain is in charge.

Nov 5th 1942 Mr Draper HMI called to see the Head Teacher about arrangements for Hot Meals in the school. He congratulated the Head Teacher on her discipline which he said "was the happy kind for which parents should be thankful." HMI kindly added that his opinion of the Head Teachers abilities were shared by his colleagues on the Inspectoral staff. HMI instructed the Head Teacher to remove the girls' cloakroom chairs which had been left there from an entertainment. He also ordered the removal of sandbags from the small from window of the classroom, and said that the scheme for hot meals would come into force as soon as the necessary structural alterations were carried out.

Nov 6th 1942 Sandbags from small window in the classroom were removed according to instructions from Mr Draper, Chief HMI for Somerset.

Summary of Managers Meeting on 21st Dec 1943:
Sanitary operation – a truck had been found for the Caretaker.
County authorities had little hope of a sign in the village to warn motorists of the school.

Circulars H1205 Award for special places for evacuee had
been received and filed.
A lot of discussion about the use of the small room as a
Wardens Post due to there being a camp bed left in there.
There was also the possibility that the room would be used
for washing up and as a canteen. The managers discussed
the canteen, their opinion that the canteen was 'by no
means generally necessary though certain children would
benefit who came from a distance.'

1943

Jan 4th 1943 School re-opened this morning, and hot meals were
served for the first time in the school canteen. Sandbags and beds
still remain, contrary to HMI's instructions. In spite of these
obstructions, the meal was very popular with the children, and the
scheme promises too be a great success. School hours now 9.30–
12.15 and 1.30–3.30.

Jan 20th 1943 Mr Draper HMI called to see the canteen. He
understood from the correspondent that the beds were now folded
up against the wall, but found this was not so. He said that it was
obviously unhealthy to have light and air excluded by dirty, useless
sandbags from a room where children had to eat, and that it was
most undesirable to have men sleeping there at night. He was very
disgusted at the lack of drainage and made notes of this. Mr
Snelgrove called in the afternoon, and told the Head Teacher of the
Chief Education Officer's reply to complaints made by a few
parents through the correspondent. He showed her a copy of the
letter, in which Mr Deacon said that the LEA regarded Mrs Coghill
as an efficient Head Teacher, who has her school well in hand, and
who is praised by the Boards Inspectors. Mr Snelgrove heard some
reading and said that there was obviously no grounds for
complaint. Mr Snelgrove said that he, as well as HMI Mr Draper,
would be pleased to recommend the Head Teacher for any post she
would care to apply in the county.

Feb 1st 1943 The Head Teacher sent in her resignation, having
been appointed Headmistress of a Grade II school in Wiltshire.

Feb 5th 1943 Miss Grant, HMI, called to tell the Head Teacher of a
vacant headship at Shapwick, and was sorry to hear that she had
already accepted a post in Wiltshire.

Feb 26th 1943 Received from County Hall - 30 tart plates and 30
dessert spoons for use in the canteen. Miss Grant HMI called the

afternoon to see whether the Wardens' beds had been removed from the canteen. She made note of the fact that they were still there, also sand bags still blocking up the window, excluding air and light. Miss Grant recommended the Head Teacher to keep the children out of doors as much as possible, in view of the prevalence of coughs and colds.

Memories of David Kingcott

I started school in 1939. The Headteacher was Mrs Coghill, Marjorie Bagg was monitor, also Mary Pearce, and later on Mrs Fountain who used to come by train from Weston. In my final years Miss Bate was Headmistress.

I lived at Ham Farm and went to school, when I was small, by horse and cart. Frank Chappell, who worked for my father, took me with the milk churns and dropped me off at the school. The milk churns were picked up from a big platform which was between Rustic Farm and the Post Office. Later I used to ride to school on the crossbar of my brother Ivor's bike or I'd walk.

The free school milk came from Richie Bagg's farm then. My friends and playmates were the Ruston girls especially Stella, who was my closest pal, also Cecil Norton.

The toilets were appalling - there were no flushes just wooden seats going down into a pit. The bell was not allowed to be rung during the wartime and no church bells either, although if there was an invasion all of the bells were to be rung to warn people. At the end of the war, I used to ring it in my last year as my great-grandfather had presented it to the school. It was rung 5 minutes before school started. The rope came down into the large room by the window, it had an end like the bell ropes in the church. The well at the school was not fit to be used so water was fetched from Court House – two big boys took a bucket and drew water each day from the well there, the nearest fresh water spring was at Kingston Bridge.

During the war a telephone was put into the small classroom for the warden on fire duty. The unexploded bomb, which closed the school, was in the village between the council houses and the Triangle in a watering. People living in the Triangle had to be evacuated. When school finally reopened, I remember going with other children to see the very deep crater where it had been dug out. I also remember a large bomb dropping half way between Middle Lane Farm and Brittons Farm where my Grandparents lived; it was a large sea mine and the chains on it made a loud clanking noise as it came down. The large explosion blew out windows and some ceilings collapsed in the back of Brittons Farm. Fortunately, the front of the house was not damaged.

Mrs Coghill had a big brightly coloured parrot, it used to sit in its cage by the window facing the road. A girl put her finger through the cage once and got bitten; it bled rather a lot and made a beak shaped mark on her finger; she was very upset!

On a summer's afternoon Mrs Coghill would sometimes take us to sit on the School House lawn and read books to us. Plays were held in the school occasionally or on the Rectory lawn. The Reverend Gornall and his wife were very keen on dramatic things and helped out – she was very lady-like. I was the King in *Sleeping Beauty*. I had to say, "Flip, darn, botheration, I forgot your invitation!" – I remember everyone laughing. The school was let out sometimes as there was no village hall. A Land Girl with the Powells organised some amateur dramatics called *Crackerjacks*. Socials were also held in the school. We used to see information films in the evening, usually followed by a cartoon. Some mothers wrote letters as they weren't very happy with the education of their children. Mrs Coghill left soon after, very upset. I enjoyed Mrs Coghill and was very sorry when she left. On the whole, I was happy at Kingston School.

Extract from Managers Minutes 2nd March 1943: An emergency meeting. Mrs Coghill's letter of resignation. Application from Miss E.G.Bate. After reading Miss Bate's accomplishments and testimonials as a teacher during the last 26 years, it was decided to recommend Miss Bate.

Mar 5th 1943 The County Examinations for special places in primary schools was held today. Three candidates were present out of six the others being absent through sickness.

Mar 29th 1943 Mrs Fountain resumed duty today. Two boxes of books received from County Library. PC Claxton called with the GWR lorry-driver to see whether contents of a parcel containing school stationery were intact. This parcel had been tampered with in transit, but nothing was missing.

Apr 20th 1943   HMI Miss Grant called to say "Goodbye" to the Head Teacher. She expressed her regret that the Head Teacher was leaving Somerset, and thanked her for her work in the County. Miss Peake, County Inspector, sent the Head Teacher a letter recording her appreciation of the work done in the last six years, and recording the fact that this school is 'being handed over in excellent working order.' (copy in Report File)

Apr 21st 1943   Attendances for April 719 = av. of 25.
In making my last entry in this book, I desire to wish my successor every happiness in her work here, and to record my appreciation of the happy, friendly spirit of the children. I am also grateful to my colleague Mrs DM Fountain, for her unswerving loyalty in this difficult time.   M Coghill Headmistress 1937-1943.

Chapter 11
Miss Bate

Extract from Managers Minutes 18th March 1943:

Miss EG Bate appointed as Mistress. Seeing that the School House will not be occupied by the Headmistress on this occasion, it was proposed that the house be offered to Mr Sedgbeer at 10/- a week... Also partitioning separating the Infant' play ground from the rest should come down – the school had no longer senior children.

Extracts from a letter sent to Joan Ridley from Gordon and Elizabeth Cullen (Sedgbeer) and John Sedgbeer following the open day and cream tea in the school during the summer of 2003:

Our visit evoked many memories, not least for me of laying in bed at School House and listening to the music for the Barn Dance, Valetta, Gay Gordons, etc. each time there was a dance or party at the school. On the night of a Beetle Drive my doll's cups were frequently used to shake the dice if they didn't have enough eggcups! Another event was a Bell-ringers' Breakfast, I think it was. Mum, Gran and Mrs Norton cooked it at School House and served it in the schoolroom.

Seeing the weavers' work on display reminded me of all the raffia baskets which Miss Bate used to display at the annual 'Sale of Work'. I remember all the articles either knitted or sewed and cakes, jams, pickles etc. and Granny Harris serving tea and cakes – just like last Saturday in the smaller classroom.

I found it quite nostalgic – with the special thoughts of my parents at School House and all my friends who came to play, Granny and Grandpa Palmer at Rectory Cottage and all the hard work they did as caretakers of both school and church, of them lighting the coke stoves so that at least the chill was taken from the air by the time children arrived at School – never adequate in the main room.

May 4th 1943   Today I begin my duties as Headmistress of this school.
Eleanor Gertrude Bate 19/19161
Note: Miss Bate lived at Myrtle Cottage with her sister.

June 9th 1943   This school was closed today for the children's Concert in connection with Wings for Victory Week.

Sept 3rd 1943   Today being the National Day of Prayer, the children attended a service in church in place of the usual lesson of religious instruction.

Oct 12th 1943 Mrs Vawdrey RSPCA visited this school today and presented prizes for essays written. The Prize winners being Royston Wallis; Nancy Jones; Hilda Bowdrey and May Ruston.

1944

> *Extract from Managers Minutes 19th March 1944:*
> *Pictures of the Holy Family purchased but awaiting frames. The L.E.A. disclaimed ownership of the harmonium.*
> *Mrs Palmer the cleaner after 29 – 30 years has sent her resignation. Mrs Fountain's duties terminated, the reason that evacuees from London had dropped to almost vanishing point.*
> *The Youth Club had paid for the use of the schoolroom (1/- a night) for November 1st to January 26th.*

May 2nd 1944 Mrs Fountain left today to take up her new appointment. Miss Hilda Mabel Claydon has been temporarily appointed in her place.

July 25th 1944 PC Claxton called and talked to the children about the danger of picking up any queer looking objects.

Sept 29th 1944 The (RSPCA) prize winners were:-
Nancy Jones; Mary Sims; Ray Stuckey and Brian Griffin.
1945

> *Extract from Manager's Minutes 8th Jan 1945   Proposed scullery in connection with the children's Canteen. It was pointed out that probably for a Parish use, the size and position of the scullery would be of little value.*

1945

Jan 26th 1945 The bad snowy weather continued and only 15 out of 31 children came. We had morning school but, as no dinners came, we were forced to go home at 1 o'clock and, as the children came from such long distances, they could not return in the afternoon. Miss Claydon was ill and could not come.

Jan 29th 1945   Miss Claydon still unable to come   and the attendance very low 50%. The Managers decided to close the school for the rest of the week.

> *Extract from Managers' Minutes 23rd Feb 1945;*
> *A letter from LEA. The Education Authorities were ready to build a scullery, cost would be in the region of £200. The Managers decided to agree to let the LEA build the scullery*

Mar 9th 1945 Miss Orr, Inspector of Physical Training, called this morning at 11.30am and brought gym shoes for all the juniors and the top infants.

Apr 11th 1945 Miss Claydon returned but was far from well. I had an extended playtime to give her a rest.

May 8th 1945 School closed today and tomorrow for the two days V E Holiday.
Note: Victory in Europe Day marked the end of the War in Europe

Nov 2nd 1945 Mrs Vawdrey Secretary of the R.S.P.C.A. called today to present prizes for essays written earlier in the year. The prize winners were :-
Brian Griffin; Esme Jones; Nancy Jones and Pauline Neads

> *Extract from Managers Minutes 30th Nov 1945.*
> *County Architect's plans to carry out improvements at the school in accordance with the 1944 Education Act.*
> *Consideration given to the County for the Infant School in the Parish & that Juniors go to Clevedon along with the seniors. This was carried unanimously.*
> *Dec 3rd 1945 The County Committee had concluded that 'no primary school should consist of fewer than two classes: except in a few special cases where it will still be necessary to retain a one class school.'*
> *The Managers decided to recommend that Kingston would be a special case and could become a school just for Infants.*

Back Row Theodore Burdge John Summerell John Travis Cyril Simmons Graham Griffin Bruce Norton Ewen Ian Hymes Tony Chappell Sam Burdge **Middle Row** Elizabeth Sedgbeer Barbara Parsons Joan Travis Anne Wallis Christine Chappell Gillian Williams Cynthia Carpenter Monica Griffin Oliver Powell **Front Row** Michael Parsons Judith Powell Sylvia Stuckey Gerald Harris Maurice Carpenter Assistant Teacher Miss Hill (Joyce Harris Collection) **1947**

1946

May 17th 1946   The Free place examination took place today from 9.30 – 3.30pm. There was only one candidate John Sedgbeer. The invigilators were as follows:-
Mr E Harris 9.30am – 11am. Mrs E Wallis 11am – 12.30pm. Mrs E Wallis 2.00pm – 2.45pm. Mr E Griffin 2.45 – 3.30pm.
The Headteacher was present throughout as directed.

June 7th 1946   Lesson on "Safety First" given to the whole school. 23 children.

July 18th 1946   Mrs Vawdrey, Hon Sec. Of the R.S.P.C.A., visited the school at 2.45pm and presented the prizes for the essays written. The prize winners were :- Esme Jones; Brian Griffin; John Sedgbeer and Ray Chappell.

Nov 18th 1946   Miss Claydon left to be married. The Doctor called at 2.15pm for inoculations.

> *Extract from the Managers Minutes 27th Nov 1946   The Managers agreed to a Controlled Status of their School. Mrs Wallis asked the Rector to take charge of the Deeds and keep them in the safe at the Rectory.*

1947

Jan 8th 1947   The Rector called at 1.30pm and talked to the children.
Note: this would have been the new Rector the Rev. Percy William Rees Rowlands.

Feb 10th 1947   A very snowy and slippery day. No dinners arrived and so school had to be closed for the afternoon session.

Feb 12th 1947   The County Examination for special places in Secondary Schools was held today.

> *Extract from Managers Meeting 27th March 1947: The Rector briefly explained the present position regarding the school & mentioned that Mr Moody (Wells) in his reply had stated that the County could not take over the School House when it took over the school.*

May 21st 1947   Two members of the Staff of Clevedon Modern School visited us this afternoon and stayed for about half an hour.

June 23rd 1947 Miss Hill away all day owing to a poisoned foot caused by a gnat sting.

June 30th 1947 The Superintendent of the Police of Weston-super-Mare District came this morning at 10.45 am and gave a second talk upon Safety First.

Sept 8th 1947 Re-opened today after Summer Holiday – no on roll at present 19.

Nov 20th 1947 School closed for today on the occasion of the Marriage of HRH Princess Elizabeth to the Duke of Edinburgh.

Nov 26th 1947 I was away ill, the first time for 4 and half years.

Dec 19th 1947 We broke up for the Christmas Holidays and gave a Concert for the parents, managers and friends.

Memories of Kingston Seymour School 1944-50 by Anne Moore (nee Wallis) – lived at Broadstone Farm

The Headmistress was Miss G Bate. The teachers were Miss Claydon and later Mrs Hill. Both these ladies travelled daily from Weston-super-Mare; they cycled from/to Yatton Railway Station.

Pupils either walked or cycled to school. I normally cycled the one mile from Broadstone each day but in the winter of 1947 I had to walk through the snow drifts (and along the frozen rhynes!). During the most severe part of that winter, the drifts made it impossible to get to school; in fact the school was closed for a few days when the toilets were frozen.

Whenever two teachers were available, two classrooms were used. Miss Bate normally taught the older pupils in the small room, presiding over the class from a high pulpit-like desk. The other teacher took the younger ones in the larger room (the hall) where the desks occupied half of the floor space. Coats, gym shoes etc. were hung on personal pegs in the lobby and books, pencils etc, were kept in our own desks. There were shelves for a small library and a large cupboard for stationery etc. A 'Nature-table' took pride of place in the corner.

Summoned by the ringing of a bell, school commenced at nine o'clock with daily assembly conducted by Miss Bate who also played the piano. We sang a hymn, listened to a Bible story followed by a prayer and closed by reciting The Lord's Prayer.

Lessons were always interesting. Multiplication tables were a daily routine and spelling tests were held twice a week.

In the mid-morning break the appointed milk-monitors distributed the milk – 1/3rd pint to each pupil. In winter they brought the crates inside to thaw the milk by the coke-burning stove - if they were left too long, we had boiled milk!

At dinnertime, tables were erected and laid in the vacant area of the hall. Cooked dinners arrived from Yatton in vacuum containers. Stew was mainly vegetables with a little meat if we were lucky. My favourite item was steamed sponge pudding with jam of syrup and lumpy custard; those served last had most lumps!

After dinner the tables were cleared away, each pupil collected a fibre mat and lay on the floor for a nap. The oldest pupils were at the back of the room with Infants and new pupils at the front. Misbehaving pupils were also moved to the front under the teacher's beady eye.

During the afternoon we did craftwork – sewing, making small raffia mats, French knitting, etc followed by a story read to us before finishing the day. I can remember being intrigued by stories of 'Little Black Samba' who lived on a desert island and carried a water pitcher on his head.

P.E. was held in the side playground. There were team games such as Pass the Beanbag, Skipping, Hoop Races and Leap-Frog. During wet weather we stayed inside and did exercises in the hall. For all these activities it was 'dresses tucked inside knickers'!

In the summer months we went on nature walks to Wemberham Lane, each pupil collecting an assorted bunch of wild flowers and leaves to be identified on return to school. Sometimes we pressed them to make a flower book.

Christmas parties were always exciting times. We played games – pass the parcel, musical chairs, statues, etc. I remember one occasion when there was a ventriloquist with a schoolboy called Joey; we were all mesmerized by Joey actually speaking to us! Even though rationing was in operation, the food was special – sandwiches, jelly, cream and homemade cakes. Each pupil was given some chocolate with the instruction NOT to eat it on the way home. I was disobedient, ate it and was violently sick. To this day I hate Mars Bars!

The school's doctor and dentist visited periodically. Surgeries were held either in the small classroom or in School House (the home of Mrs Sedgbeer). I can still hear pupils crying after injections and the screeching dentist's drill!

Miss Bate loved flowers as witnessed by her colourful orchard in springtime with beautiful shows of daffodils, etc. at Myrtle Cottage. It really was a lovely sight as her bantam chicks scuttled amongst the blooms. Each autumn she gave every pupil a flower bulb to plant and we waited eagerly until early spring to see whose was the biggest and the best. Prizes were awarded to the winners.

Schooldays at Kingston Seymour were happy days; it was a different world when moving from a close-knit school of 30 pupils to one with over 500. However, the simple lessons of everyday village life, learnt in such a community spirit, have stood many pupils in good stead in facing whatever life had to throw at them.

1948

Jan 15th 1948   Miss Whiteley, Health Visitor, called today at 10.15am She saw all the children. Roll 23.

Feb 11th 1948   Ash Wednesday – The Rector came to address the children and took the School Service.

July 1st 1948   Sergeant Marsh of Weston-super-Mare came and gave a talk of Safety First. He also inspected the bicycles.

Nov 17th 1948   Miss Orr called and brought 19 pairs of gym shoes and ten hoops.

Extract from Managers Minutes 26th Dec 1948:
Letter from Miss Bate asking the managers to write to Mr Deacon, the Chief Education Officer & ask him if he could use his authority to get the water from the main brought on to the school while work was going on.

1949

Feb 11th 1949   The county Examination   for Free Places in Secondary Schools was held today. There were three candidates

May 31st 1949 Mr Hector, Hon. Sec. R.S.P.C.A. came to present prizes to the children for essays written. The prize winners were:- Ray Chappell, Rita Jones and John Summerell.

> *Extract from Managers Minutes 10th July 1949: Mrs Wallis asked who would have the guarantee for the Company's water when it was laid on at the school. The managers said it would be wise to mention this in her letter to Chief Education Officer.*

July 20th 1949   Mrs H St John Tomlinson called to collect the envelopes for the C of E Children's Society – our children collected £1. 9s 10d.

> *Extract from Managers Minutes Aug 29th 1949:*
> *Letters from Rev Moody (Wells) – it was resolved to ask for Controlled Status immediately. Rev Moody also asked for the Trust Deeds to be forwarded on to him. But as the Deeds include School House it was decided that Mr Moody be asked if he wished to see them, the Rev Rowlands would be pleased to show them to him anytime by appointment. It was decided to purchase a churn carrier and a churn from Mr W.R. Bailey, Congresbury, the expense to be shared by the managers & the Rev. Rowlands for the hauling of water for use of school children & the Rectory.*

Sept 5th 1949 School re-opened today at 9am. My roll is the same as last term viz 22.

Nov 24th 1949 School closed for Sale of Work in aid of Church Training Collleges for Teachers.

> *Extract from the Managers Minutes 4th December 1940:*
> *A meeting called to elect new Tenant for the School House as Mr A Sedgbeer was leaving School House to reside in Yatton. Miss Hill was then proposed to be given first chance on School House on conditions that she be willing to do certain duties.*

1950

Jan 19th 1950 Miss Westbrooke H.M.I. called this morning at 9.30am and stayed until 12.10pm. She said that the work of the School was most satisfactory.

Jan 31st 1950 Half day for Childrens' Party.

Feb 10th 1950 The County Examinations for Free Places in Secondary Schools was held today. There were five candidates, viz Anne Wallis, Graham Griffin, Anthony Chappell, Bernard Carpenter, and Bruce Norton.

Feb 22nd 1950 The Rector came to address the children for Ash Wednesday. Closed school half term and Polling Day.

Mar 17th 1950 Captain Hector of the R.S.P.C.A. came this afternoon to address the children and present prizes won for essays written last Autumn. The prize winners being: 1. Graham Griffin, 2. Barbara Parsons, 3. Elizabeth Sedgbeer.
> *Extract from Managers Minutes 15th June 1950:*
> *Mrs E Wallis's resignation from correspondentship on account of ill health. Appreciation and thanks were expressed to Mrs Wallis for her services. Miss Hill withdrew here application for School House and Miss G Benelory had taken it from Jan 8th.*

July 28th 1950 Broke up for the Summer Holiday. We gave Miss Hill a present as she is not returning after the holiday.

1951

Sept 4th 1951 Returned to school with a roll of 18. Mr Bray called.

Sept 13th 1951 Miss Painter, Meal Supervisor, called at dinner time. She said that I should try to get a dinner helper in order to have a rest.

Oct 10th 1951 Messrs Coles of West Town have started to do the playground.

1951

Jan 24th 1951 Mr Smith of Pill came to repair the stove in the small room.

1951 Bobbie Pine and Ronnie Chappell, Rodney and Angela Pine, William Travis

Feb 6th 1951   The Free Place Examination was held today. There were 3 candidates: Sonia Kilminster, Barbara Parsons and Joan Travis.

Extract from Managers Minutes 8th April 1951: Mr W.J. Hanham given up contract for transport of children. It was considered that transport was not necessary during the Summer Term but next Term 4 young children living a distance of over two miles would need transport. The managers suggested either Brian Warburton or Atlay & Son might undertake the work.

Sept 3rd 1951   Re-assembled after the summer Holidays. Roll now 23, 8 girls, 15 boys.

1952

Feb 5th 1952   The County Examination for Free Places in Secondary Schools was held today. There was only one candidate taking the examination. The other child in this age group being educationally subnormal.

June 23rd 1952   Scripture Exam – Miss Allen the Examiner.

June 27th 1952 ---- ---- most impudent. In a one teacher school, boys of this type ought to be expelled

Extract from Managers Minutes 21st April and 17th July 1952:
Resignation of Headmistress at end of August next.
Applicants for Headmistress interviewed, after subsequent deliberations Mrs Olive Griffiths of Kenn was elected unanimously.

July 25th 1952 Miss Westbrooke H.M.I Called this afternoon to wish me a happy retirement. The Rector and other school managers came this afternoon and made me a presentation on behalf of themselves and parents of past and present children.
This is the last entry I shall make after being Head Mistress for over nine years. The last two years have been very hard, the roll usually being over twenty including three subnormal children and two most unruly boys from Portishead. I wish Mrs Griffiths every success in a hard and difficult task.
E.G. Bate

Miss Bate is remembered on a plaque in Kingston Church following her death on December 18ᵗʰ 1976:

'A faithful worshipper in this church and by whose generosity this church was re-decorated and the chancel re-ordered to the memory of the late Rev. M. R. Green. This work was carried out entirely by voluntary labour by members and non-members of this church. March 1980.'

Chapter 12
Mrs Griffiths Arrives

1ˢᵗ Sept 1952   I commence duties today as Head Mistress of this
school. Numbers on Roll 18.
 O Griffiths

*Note: Mrs Olive Griffiths lived in the School House at Kenn and
had been Headmistress of that School during the War, when Kenn
School closed she was appointed to Kingston School. Some of the
children from Kenn travelled on the bus with her every day.
Mrs Griffiths eventually moved to Clevedon to live.*

**John Wallis was at the school when the new headmistress took
over:**

**"I don't remember too much about this time but I do know
that my fingers never stopped stinging! Miss Bate had never
used corporal punishment on the pupils; she tried to control
them verbally. Things had got a bit out of hand towards the
end of her time. Some children took advantage and were very
unruly. Mrs Griffiths started off as she intended to continue.
She had to be very strict to make her mark. To be fair, once
she had the school under control, she was a good teacher."**

> *Extract from Managers Minutes 3ʳᵈ Sept 1952:*
> *Mr and Mrs Palmer resigned as school cleaners, it was
> suggested that Mrs Stansfield be asked to do the cleaning,
> Mrs S Griffin the meals and Mrs Hanham the offices.*

Nov 28ᵗʰ 1952   School closed for the day. Head Teacher absent
with vocal trouble.

Dec 1ˢᵗ 1952   School re-opened. Roads are frozen and transport is
difficult but 17 children are present out of 19.

Dec 19ᵗʰ 1952   School play and party.

1953

Jan 7ᵗʰ 1953   The new dinner supervisor Mrs Kellow commenced
duties today.

Jan 14th 1953   Miss Grant H.M.I. visited the school and discussed with the Head Teacher her needs, books, etc. So many books left in cupboards are very old. Head Teacher had brought some books from her old school at Kenn which had been closed.
Miss Grant made an allowance of £5 for extra requisition of books.

Jan 23rd 1953   A surveyor from the County Architects Office in Taunton called about the school water supply. The water pipe is now as far as the Rectory, and is to be brought across the road to the school.

Feb 3rd 1953 School closed for the day (one teacher of 22 children) to enable arrangements to be made for three children to sit the County Free Place Examination. The Rev. PWR Rowlands, invigilated all day from 9.30-3.30pm. I was present the whole day.

Feb 18th 1953 Ash Wednesday. Rev PW.R. Rowlands, the Rector, called at school and took an Ash Wednesday Service with the children, instead of scripture. In the afternoon H.M. Inspector called at the school and inspected dinner arrangements. She suggested a wooden 'trip board' at the kitchen sink.

Mar 9th 1953 Miss Childs, Meals Supervisor, called and stayed to see children take dinner. Remarked on the improved discipline and orderly, happy behaviour of the children at dinnertime. Several children absent owing to sickness, 17 present out of 22. Miss Childs will enquire will enquire again as to delay in getting the water laid on at school from the Rectory.

Mar 20th 1953 Attendance down to 54% owing to measles, mumps and influenza, wrote to the chief education officer about the school water supply, as the rain-water supply has dried up this fortnight, and all water for the canteen, washing up, as well as drinking water has to be carried from the village.
Note: there was a stand-pipe in the Triangle in front of the War Memorial. People from all around the village would go there, often with milk churns, to fill up with drinking water. A special "key" was used to turn on the supply.

May 1st 1953 Pipe measured from the Rectory for connecting the school for drinking water. Estimates sent to the Chief Education Officer.

Extract from Manager Minutes 3rd May:

A meeting to discuss the water situation at the school. Now that three different persons did the work formerly done by a husband and wife there was a certain amount of friction as to whose duty it was to fetch the water. It was proposed that a letter be sent to the Education Committee urging them to reconsider their decision about having the water installed.

May 14th 1953 School closed for half day holiday. Number present 8 out of 22 owing to measles and suspects for same. Notifies the Rector who telephoned Taunton, and received instructions to keep the school open (new regulations).

May 22nd 1953 School closed for Whitsun Holidays one week, and three days holiday June 1st – 3rd for the Coronation of Queen Elizabeth II. Attendance still low. 7 out of 22, owing to Measles Epidemic.

Kingston School John Harris 1951- 57

M is for *Memories*: crates of 1/3 pint bottles of *Milk* thawing out beside the coke stove; *Marbles* during playtime – I still have a large biscuit tin of 'bloodhounds'; *Music and Movement* on the Home Service; *Mrs Griffiths* – the Welsh dragon who to me was kindness itself (creep) and *Miss* Purkis – say no more about the childish jokes!

Nature walks around the village in which we as country children taught Mrs Griffiths far more than she ever taught us. We, whose birds' eggs collections would now be illegal, whose moles at 9d per skin went heaven knows where. Eddie Baker used to collect the infants from the outlying farms in an Atlay's taxi. John Wallis and I cycled. A stone removed from atop the railings at the end of Yeo Bank Lane meant one of the other had given up waiting. We stored our bikes at "Uncle Edgar's" (Wallis, Cherry Tree Farm).

I was never a fan of school lunches and rebelled in my last year, cycling home for a meal instead. But overall, fond memories of the school, my sister Ann and brother Brian joining me there before moving on. And moving on to what? I hadn't realised the importance of the 11 plus when I took it – it was the full frontal bear hug out in the road from Olive Griffiths that told me I had passed. My first lesson at

Crewkerne School, a boarding Grammar, was Greek and it was only then that I learnt what a verb was, and the naivety of my education up to that point.

Kingston Seymour V.C. School was simple and basic, but it did me proud!

July 15th 1953   School closed for the afternoon for the school outing to Bristol Zoo.

July 22nd 1953 ----- ---- fell in the school yard and hit his head. He collided with two boys coming round the corner. I bathed his head and sent him home in the school car, and sent a note to parent. Called at his home later and explained to parent it was quite accidental.

July 24th 1953 ----- ----- bitten by a dog on the way to school. I reported to the farmer and put Dettol and a pad on the bite. Reported to parent and suggested ---- should be taken to the Doctor for an injection.

Sept 28th 1953 On trying to open school window it slammed on my hands, the cords were broken. My fingers were crushed and I left school to have them dressed by a nurse, and then was examined by Dr Kilvert of Clevedon. I reported to Rev P.W.R. Rowlands and he telephoned County Ed. Officer and closed school for the afternoon.

Sept 29th 1953 I returned to school as my fingers are crushed and bruised but not broken. The Rector has asked for the window to be repaired.
(Note: These last two entries written in a slightly erratic hand – obviously the fingers had trouble holding the pen)

Oct 1st 1953 Mrs G Meek takes up her duties as Dinner Supervisor in place of Mrs Kellow who has been ill.

It was this winter that the original village hall was built. It was an old Army hut and was brought by Mr Bailey from Brislington to Kingston and erected on the site of the present hall. There was then no further need to rent the schoolroom for any functions.

1954

Jan 4th 1954 School re-opened. Two children admitted. Number on books 25, one teacher school.

Jan 21st 1954 Wood delivered – 4 baskets.

Jan 25th 1954 One boy sat the Preliminary Simplex Junior Intelligence Paper.

Feb 10th 1954 Used the wireless in school for the first time for music and movement. I raised funds for the school in December for Christmas Party and to purchase the wireless for school. The children are very enthusiastic about the school wireless programmes.

May 11th 1954 Reported to the Chief Education Officer that the 'Grease Trap' in children's playground is choked and flooding into the school yard. Also reported to Correspondent.

Aug 31st 1954 Climbing apparatus has been installed in the schoolyard in the holidays. Miss Orr, Physical Training Organiser, called at school and inspected the 'Climbing Apparatus'.

Sept 27th 1954 Miss Whiteley, Health Visitor, called at school and inspected children. Miss Timpson H.M.I. visited school and inspected children's work and school premises. Miss Timpson remarked on the large number of children aged 5-6 years (16) in a one teacher school.

Nov 23rd 1954 Miss Grant H.M.I. visited the school and checked the number on the Register - 29, and praised the work of the children. Miss Grant said Head Teacher working very hard single-handed with 29 children. 16 of which are infants between 5 and 6 years, working in separate room in three groups, she strongly recommends that an addition to the Staff be made to help the Head Teacher.

There is a very friendly atmosphere prevalent in the school, and some good work is in progress. P.S. Allen Ass Dir. of Religious Education

1955

Feb 1st 1955 Three children sat the County Examinations for Allocation to Secondary School. Correspondent and school manager's wives helped the Headmistress with invigilation. 9.30 – 12.30 School Correspondent Miss Bate, 2 – 3.45 Mrs B Harris, 3.45 – 4.10 Mrs Norton. I was present throughout the day.

Mar 23rd 1955 Notified from Taunton that ------ will be called for Interview, re-Free Place Examination Scholarship about April 26th.

Notified by the Chief Education Officer that an assistant teacher has been allowed for this school. Reported to the school Correspondent the dangerous state of the fence around the school playground.

Extract from Managers Minutes 22nd April 1955: A meeting to elect County Representatives. It was proposed that Mrs J Travis should be re-elected and Mrs F Kingcott be elected to take the place of Mrs D Wallis who had left the Parish.

Apr 25th 1955 Mrs A. Wright commenced duties today as a supply teacher, while an extra teacher for the infants is awaited.

May 26th 1955 Closed for General Election.

June 24th 1955 School Roll is now 31.

July 7th 1955   School closed for the School Annual Outing to Bristol Clifton Zoo.

Aug 29th 1955 School re-opened. Miss E Purkis commenced duties as Infants Teacher today. Margaret Elizabeth Purkis 53/18287.

1956

Feb 15th 1956   School closed for teachers to attend at Weston-super-Mare on Thursday and Friday Feb 16th and 17th.

Mar 9th 1956 Mrs O Griffiths left school early this afternoon with School Managers' permission to attend Redland High School extension ceremony by Sir Oliver Franks.

Mar 14th 1956 Miss M Purkis Infant Teacher, away all day, with School Managers' permission to visit East Harptree Junior School with a party of Teachers.

Apr 6th 1956 Report by H.M.I. Miss Timpson on her visit to the school on January 26th & 27th 1956:

The last report on Kingston Seymour Church of England School was made in 1937. There are now 30 names on roll. The accommodation consist of two classrooms of areas 600 and 300 square feet, a small scullery and two cloakrooms each with one washbasin. Swanmore sanitation is provided. The means of ventilating the large classroom are insufficient and in dull weather the natural lighting is inadequate. One of two electric lighting points is used to connect the wireless set. Better storage provision and wall fittings for display purposes are necessary. An overhaul of the furniture and interior redecoration might well be undertaken as soon as possible; a general higher standard of cleanliness might then be maintained. A greater variety of teaching equipment is needed and some, which is worn out, should be replaced.

The Infants Class of 15 children is taken by a teacher appointed in September 1955 to this her first appointment after training. Informal methods are employed and the children make satisfactory progress in learning the beginnings of Arithmetic and Reading. They enjoy singing and dramatising stories and rhymes. A greater variety of equipment for Art, Crafts and for other practical interests would lead to the necessary expansion of the work.

The Headmistress appointed in 1952 takes the Junior Classes in the small room, part of which is occupied by a large heating stove. It is difficult in such cramped quarters to attempt practical work on a reasonably large scale, in Art and Crafts or even adequately to show specimens for nature study. Methods of group and individual teaching is employed and the curriculum is carefully organised. The children make satisfactory progress each according to his own ability. It is a tribute to the school that the oldest pupils show themselves to be most competent in the duties they undertake during the daily programme. They are courteous, friendly and fluent in conversation.

The range of ability among the children in this small school is wide. Some of them need special encouragement to awaken their interest and to develop their powers of concentration. Clean, attractively decorated and well-fitted and equipped classrooms would be of considerable help to the Headmistress and Assistant whose tasks are by no means easy.

July 5th 1956 School Holiday – School Outing to Cheddar.

Extract from Managers Minutes 23 July 1956: Mr and Mrs Stansfield were leaving the parish. A new Caretaker would have to be appointed. There was only one person who could undertake the work and that was Mrs Neath who lives near the school.

July 26th 1956 The children gave an entertainment in the Rectory Garden, Songs, Mimes, and a Physical Training display.

The Rector and Mrs Rowlands thanked Mrs Griffiths, the Headmistress, and Miss Purkis, the Assistant teacher, for an enjoyable afternoon's entertainment. The parents showed very hearty appreciation.

Nov 22nd 1956   Report on Religious Instruction by Prebendary Franklin:

This is my first visit to the School, I was pleased with the opening worship and found the children very reverent. They are taught to be silent which is excellent. The infants are a pleasing group who respond well. The Juniors are particularly well informed.

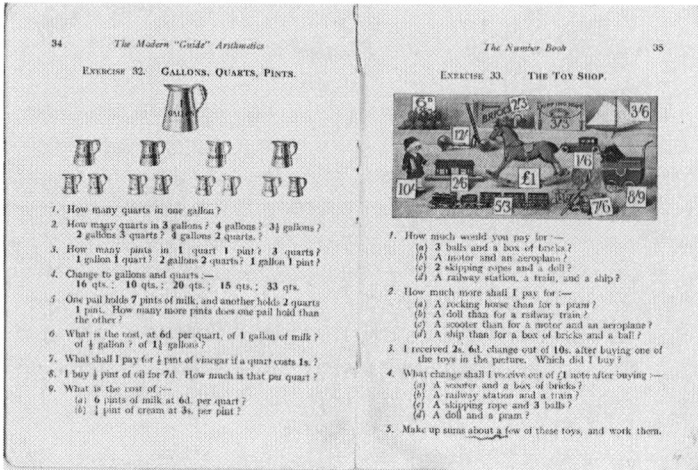

1957

Jan 14th 1957   School re-opened after three weeks instead of a fortnight, because of the petrol and fuel shortage. Number on books 32, two entrants. Decorators still working in Headmistress' room. All classes working in the large room.

Mar 20th 1957 12 children absent Whooping Cough. Percentage of attendants 62.5%. Reported to Chief School Medical Officer. *Extract from Managers Minutes 31st March: A letter from the Education Committee about the conversion of the school offices into a water carriage system & a plan studied passed by the County Architect. The Managers agreed this would be a great improvement.* (Note: This translates as having flush toilets for the children!)

Youth club outing to Barry 1960s
Sylvia Stuckey Gillian Williams ?--- Michael Parsons Tony Chappell Judy Hucker
David Hucker Roy Cole Graham Parsons Harold Wilson Joan Travis Monica Griffin
Bruce Norton Brian Griffin Theodore Burdge Cyril Simmons

Some School photographs

Norman and Tim Harris

Phillip Lampert aged 4

Brian John and Ann Harris

School outing to Burnham-on-Sea 1955
Back Row Colin Stuckey Ron Chappell John Wallis Sylvia Stuckey Olive Griffiths
Rodney Veale Pat Griffin Janet Griffin
Front Row John Harris Tim Harris Howard Parsons Mervyn Baker Rosie
Neath Elizabeth Holtham Sheila Hitchcock Anne Harris Robert Bryce
Kathleen Neath Norman Harris Jennifer Hitchcock (M Baker)

Sunday School outing to Wells circa 1959
(Joyce Harris Collection)

Memories of Roland Griffin who was at the school during the late 1950s

One of the things that I remember is playing marbles in the playground. On one occasion another boy bet all of his money that I wouldn't hit his marble, as it was quite a long distance away. By sheer luck I did, and I will always remember the look of ' what do I do now?' on his face. I always looked forward to the nature walks down the lanes and by the rhynes. I remember the milk, in the winter it was brought into the classroom to warm up and sometimes would 'go off'.

About 15 years ago in the ditch, near my garden at the back of the school, I found a writing slate. It had the name Mary Griffin written on it and she was my father's cousin! Over the years I have found several bits of broken slate in that same place so I think it was a rubbish dump for the school. At the back of the school, another time, a chap with a metal detector dug up 5 old copper pennies, they looked as though they had been placed carefully in a pile, maybe they were hidden there by a child who meant to retrieve them at a later time.

My grandfather Ernest Griffin was one of 8 boys and had one sister, they probably attended Kingston School. After the Maynards bought Riverside Farm, he was the manager of the shop and dairy there in the early 1900s. My father Reg, who was born in 1906, attended the school and later farmed at Hope Farm where we were brought up.

June 27th 1957 John Harris given leave of absence from school to attend for an interview at Bristol University before a 'Boarding School Panel'.

July 17th 1957 John Harris notified that he had gained a Free Place at Crewkerne Grammar School as a boarder.

July 18th 1957 The Junior children performed a Three Act Play, Robin Hood at the Village Hall and the Infants children several Playlets, and the parents were invited, to mark the centenary of the School. The Headmistress and the Infants Teacher were thanked by the Rector. The parents presented the Headmistress with a bouquet to show their appreciation by her and her staff. The weather was too wet for the Social Afternoon to be held in the Rectory Garden.

Oct 25th 1957 Attendance fallen to 6 children and one teacher absent with influenza. School closed for the day.

Dec 18th 1957 School Christmas Party. 40 children and 3 School Managers and friends were entertained to tea. The Rector was unable to attend.

1958

Jan 24th 1958 Attendance low in the Infants room, 8 present out of 15 owing to snow and ice conditions of the roads. Number present in the Junior room 14 out of 17.

Feb 6th 1958   Notified by the Chief Education Officer that the Intelligence Paper of the Free Place, must be done again on 18th Feb 1958, owing to a 'leakage' of this paper in the Press, before the Examination on 28th January. 2 pupils from the school will sit a second intelligence paper......

> *Extract from Managers Minutes 21st April: It was suggested to widen the entrance gates into the school yard as large coal lorries etc. could hardly get in. Mrs J Travis raised the question of a First Aid Box for the school.*

June 2nd 1958 PT Ladders delivered and used for the first time.

July 23rd 1958 School closed for School Picnic and Cricket Match in the field.

Sept 1st 1958 Present 31. Miss Purkis, now Mrs Caton, married in holidays.

> *Extract from Managers' Minutes 28th Sept 1958:   Mr Brown, the tenant of the school house, strongly objects to the idea of having three septic tanks in his garden. He has suggested the alternative scheme. Approval of Mrs Griffiths giving the Denominational Religious Instruction.*

Nov 21st 1958 Notified from County Office, Taunton, that the official name of the school is now: Kingston Seymour C of E School Primary. Official Ministry of Education Number – 3073. School wood delivered 4 Baskets.

Dec 5th 1958 School closed for one day, Queen's visit to Bristol.

Memories of Liz Pickford (Holtham)
1953 - 1960

I was 4 years old when I started at Kingston school, Kenn having closed the previous year. Mum made me a grey pinafore and one pink and one red blouse. For 'gymnastics' on a mat in the playground we stripped to voluminous knickers and rubber buttoned vests.

The predominant memory of the school is Mrs Griffiths, of course. She had no favourites – she just disliked some children more than others. I travelled from Kenn on the bus with her and 3 or 4 other Kennites. Coming home the bus waited at Kingston Triangle – how big that seemed – for about 5 minutes and Mrs G was always late for it. I was told to make the driver wait for her and I still feel the fear and dread that the bus would leave without her. As soon as I was big enough, I borrowed sister Ann's bike and cycled to school, racing the bus home.

The Library cupboard was in the infants' room and I was in charge of choosing and delivering books for villagers. They weren't allowed near the cupboard. Goodness knows what they thought of my choice; Mrs G told me on occasion I'd got it wrong but I was still left to it.

There was a succession of brave, young assistant teachers – always female – who taught the infants and played piano for assembly. I can only remember Miss Purkis who, I think, married and came back for a while.

Dinner arrived in the Dinner-Van in big aluminium trays. It always seemed nice. Tables were laid in the infants' room while Mrs G ate alone in the senior room. There was a little kitchen and we made Mrs G a pot of tea in the afternoon. There was the 1/3 pt of milk at break – curdled in summer, frozen in winter and one bottle saved for the pot of tea.

The seasons and months were marked by Shell posters being changed. They were kept in the same cupboard as the blue-black inkbottle. Nibs and ink were all rationed. Playground games seemed to have seasons as well, marbles and French knitting with cotton reels being two of them. The nit-nurse came periodically and Dr Cook, all tweeds and brogues, once a year. All lined up in knickers and vests again. Mr Scull (Skull to us) the dentist made regular visits. The chair was set up in the senior room and in we all went. I remember once going to the toilet block – earth closets in a wooden hut – and there was a pile of milk teeth in one of them. There are other things I can recall, sports day on the last day, the bars in the playground, the Japanese Anemones growing along the back wall, Mrs G's spaniel Valda, the aeroplane skimming the chimneys and frightening us all.

I could read when I started school and an older girl showed me how to knit. I can remember Ann Harris and I doing 'Comprehension' with sheets torn from educational journals, but I cannot remember actually being taught anything!

1959

Apr 13th 1959 School re-opened, two children admitted. Number on books 36.

Apr 17th 1959 Dr Cooke, School Medical Officer called at school and gave Polio injections to 13 children.

Apr 29th 1959 Reported to School Medical Officer at Taunton, a case of Scarlet Fever.

May 5th 1959 Peat delivered to school lavatories from Eclipse Peat Company, Bridgwater.

May 15th 1959 Low attendance owing to second outbreak of Scarletina and heavy colds and sore throats.

June 1st 1959 I return to duty today after being absent one week with Bronchitis and Laryngitis. Firm from Littlehampton commenced work on school lavatories.

June 5th 1959 School closed for day for Headmistress to take a party of older children to Bath and West Show at Yeovil.

June 19th 1959   Number present 19 out of 35. Outbreak of Measles. Today's percentage 54%.
Found Girl's Cloakroom swarming with maggots. Traced a 'bad smell' to the school roof, and the school cleaner's husband, W Neath, reported dead rats and dead birds 'pulsefying' (sic) under the school roof tiles. He cleaned them out and disinfected roof and cloakroom. Reported matter to the Chief Education Officer.

6th July Report on Scripture by the Diocesan Inspector, Miss Jones. The Act of Worship taken by the Headmistress was based on that set for Wednesday in the Somerset Service Book. St Richard's Prayer was chanted quietly, suitable prayers were said, some by the Headmistress alone, while the children joined in others. Two Hymns were sung, one by the infants alone. They also said a prayer by themselves for a few minutes. The whole Service was impressive and reverently carried out.

The juniors responded well to questions asked, their answers indicated careful teaching. I very much liked a Group Study Book, which is being compiled on the Parish Church. Great interest is shown in this, and it is evident that the children know a lot about their church and church life. Many are members of St Michael's Guild. The parts of the Catechism tested were well known and good answers were given on the chief sacraments.

Expression work is good and I was pleased with the fretwork models of Easter and Christmas, and a flannel graph illustrating Baptism.

It is clear a lot of thought and preparation is devoted to the spiritual side of the School's life, and the Headmistress deserves to be recommended for her work.

July 25th 1959 School closed for Midsummer Vacation five weeks. Mrs Caton, *(Miss Purkis)* Infant Teacher left today. She is moving away from the district as her husband has qualified at Bristol University. The children and Headmistress presented her with a parting gift.

Aug 31st 1959 School re-opened after Summer Holidays. Number on books 32. Miss Hawkins, Infant Teacher commenced duties today. School toilets (water flush) and new basins used for the first time. The contractors have finished the work.

Sept 3rd 1959 The matter of the school offices had been satisfactorily settled with Mr Brown and the work completed.

Oct 8th 1959 School closed for Parliamentary Election.

The School reunion brought back some memories for Janet Burdge (Stuckey)

Reciting times tables in the big school room, making paper chains and singing 'O little town of Bethlehem' before Christmas – (I think I was Mary one year); later on with the 'Big' children in the small classroom decorated with Shell nature posters. Using ink-wells and scratchy pens and copying

writing; milk breaks. We read stories and learnt poetry. I remember 'The Village Blacksmith' but if you were slow to learn, Mrs Griffiths encouraged you by rapping you across the knuckles or poking you with a pencil. I didn't suffer it too much as I enjoyed reading and writing but I was no good at mental arithmetic.

We were taken to the Church for occasions like Ascension Day. Nature walks also throughout the summer, it seemed strange to walk past our farm and have things pointed out that I knew. We brought back chestnuts and leaves which went on the 'nature table', I can remember playing marbles in the school yard, games like catch and giggles when goose grass or 'sticky love' was put on you, as you were caught. I passed my 11 plus but failed my interview for Nailsea Grammar School, probably because I was shy but didn't look too good either having fallen down in the school yard the day before and scraped my face.

The school was used for voting at General Elections and so we children had a day's holiday. I remember because one year it fell on my birthday October 8th.

Oct 9th 1959 School re-opened. Mrs Meek terminated her duties at School today, as General Assistant after six years. The children and teacher and Headmistress, presented her with a parting gift. She is leaving the district.

Oct 12th 1959 Mrs Neath, school cleaner, takes up her duties today, as Dinner General Assistant.

Oct 16th 1959 Miss Orr, County Physical Training Organiser called at school and inspected Physical Training, and expressed her approval of the activities and praised groups for very good work, and said they were all very keen, and were using the apparatus very well, and the 'finishing off', of the exercises was neat. She advised the new Infant Teacher, Miss Hawkins, on the active approach to the work.

Dec 16th 1959 Children performed Christmas Plays and Items for parents and friends at school, the Rector's wife (Mrs Rowlands) thanked the Headmistress and presented gifts to the staff. Mr P Harris, on behalf of the parents, thanked the Headmistress.

Chapter 13
The Sixties & Closure

1960

Feb 2nd 1960   7 children sat the Free Place Examination to Grammar Schools.

Mar 9th 1960 A visitor from the County Office, Architect's Dept. called and measured school kitchen. Complained to him about the smell in the sink in the kitchen.

May 5th 1960 School closed tomorrow, 6th May, for the wedding of H.R.H. Princess Margaret, a school holiday. Number on books 31.

May 27th 1960 School closed for school outing to Windsor and The Thames.

July 14th 1960 Children performed two plays at the Village Hall to a very appreciative audience of mothers and fathers. The Rector thanked the Headmistress and her assistant for an enjoyable performance and presented them with gifts from the parents.

Extract from Manager's Minutes 1st Oct 1960: Concern was expressed about the bus, and the managers were anxious that the children should have the full school hours as required by Court. Enquiries to be made.

Further extract from 22nd January 1961: Mrs J Travis proposed that Mrs F Kingcott should be elected as correspondent. Repairs urgently needed to the school fabric.

1961

Feb 15th 1961 The children attended Service at Church, Ash Wednesday, instead of Scripture Lesson.

June 20th 1961 School closed 20 and 21st June for School Outing to Totnes and Paignton.

July 20 1961   A man from the County Surveyor's Office called at School and inspected the rhynes near the School which are unpleasant.

July 28th 1961   The Headmistress presented Miss M Hawkins, the Infant's Teacher, with a wedding present from the children and herself. Miss Hawkins terminates her duties today at this school. School closed for Midsummer Vacation, five weeks.

Sept 4th 1961   Mrs J Davies, Infants Teacher, takes up duties at school, today.

Dec 22nd 1961   Poor attendance for the last four weeks of term owing to influenza and sickness among the children. Children had a School Xmas Party as usual.

1962

Feb 5th 1962   Film Show of British Railways at the School at 7pm to decide about School Outing to London. About 70 parents, children, friends and teachers attended. The evening was thoroughly enjoyed.

Sue Thomas (Travis) remembers the excitement of recognising the 'School Outing Man' when he came into the classroom to see Mrs Griffiths, "we knew an outing was going to be arranged. He seemed to come every year".

> *On the 22nd May 1962 the managers received the news that the school would eventually be closed. They decided to send a letter to the County with reasons why this should not happen.*

June 1st 1962   School closed for School Outing to Oxford and Blenheim Palace. Party of 28 children. Teachers and parents had a very happy and interesting time.

July 27th 1962   Four boys leave today, one to Nailsea Grammar School and three to Clevedon Secondary Modern School – the new school in Swiss Valley, Clevedon.

Oct 23rd 1962   Miss Childs, Dinner Organiser, visited school and inspected the serving of the school dinners.

Nov 20th 1962   New school piano delivered.

Dec 18th 1962 School children performed their Christmas Plays to parents and friends and school managers. The entertainment was concluded with Carol Singing. The Headmistress and Infant's Teacher Mrs Davies, were thanked by the parents, who showed great appreciation. Afterwards parents and friends were shown the children's decorations made for the School Party Tables and to take home. They were delighted with the Christmas candle, table decorations and hanging glitter boughs.

1963

Jan 7th 1963 School not re-opened by instruction from Chief Ed. Officer owing to the severe snowy weather. All roads to K.S. blocked with snow. The School toilets and water pipes are frozen.

Jan 14th 1963   School Re-opened half the children away with chicken pox. Toilets still frozen, but drinking water pipes in school kitchen have been thawed. The schoolyard is in a bad condition with frozen snow and ice. The roads to the village are very frozen and dangerous. The buses will not run to the village, both teachers are walking 1¼ miles from the 'Bridge' to get to school. School is closed daily at 2.45pm No playtime or 'dinner hour' play. Children have dinners served as usual. The school car comes at 2.30pm to take the younger children home to the outlaying farms. Transport is very difficult.

Jan 24th 1963 School closed today and Friday – no coke. School toilets still frozen and schoolyard full of ice and snow.

Jan 28th 1963 School re-opened. Coke supply delivered. Keeping the electric water heater on in the school kitchen to keep tops from freezing. Some children still away with chicken pox.

Feb 20th 1963 New electric water heater installed on kitchen wall. Toilets still frozen, but yard cleared of snow.

Marion Pudner (Kingcott):
My memories of the winter of 1963

One of the most outstanding enjoyable periods of my childhood was the winter of 1963, the year I took my 11-Plus. It started snowing on Boxing Day, and within days roads were blocked, snow had drifted into high mounds and the rhynes and ponds were deeply frozen. In those days, the winter water level in the rhynes was kept much higher than now. If you fell through the

ice there would have been three or four feet of water underneath.

My aunt who lived on the Mendips and worked at Weston came to stay overnight at Christmas and didn't get back home for six weeks! My mother took her to Yatton station each day to catch the train to work. The main roads, as I remember, were fairly passable eventually, but for weeks Kingston lanes remained very treacherous and difficult to drive along.

I think we were usually dropped off at school by car and then walked home as school was let out early. I remember the worry of my parents when once I was very late home after walking through the snow around the lanes by Yew Tree Farm. It was always a disappointment that we had no hills to go sledging down - this being pre motorway bridge days - but some of the boys made a slide down the side of the rhyne bank which had to suffice. I also remember one of them trying to ride a bike on the ice.

Things that stand out are playing on the frozen rhynes and ditches as we walked home from school, cold sunny days; frozen cold fingers in sodden woollen gloves - my mother must have had a job to supply enough dry ones; having snowball fights; being careful not to go too close to the side of the bridges and gouts where the ice might be thin, and playing with friends, Kathleen Wallis, Sue Travis, Margaret Stuckey, Graham and Valerie Parsons; making snow dens in the ditches.

My parents always seemed to be cheerful with us although things must have been very difficult for them as farmers. The milk churns had to be taken to the village Triangle for the lorry to pick up there, the ice broken on the waterings for animals still in the fields and water pipes had to be thawed out daily. The mains water supply to the cow houses at Ham Farm was completely frozen for several weeks. Feeding the stock and just keeping young children warm and well fed must have taken considerable energy.

The long cold spell seemed to go on forever. It is a tribute to Mr and Mrs Neath that they kept the stoves alight and that I don't ever remember being cold in school during this time.

Mar 4th 1963 The school photographer called at school and took the children's photographs.

Mar 14th 1963 Attended a Managers Meeting to discuss the future of the school as the Infants Teacher is to be withdrawn at the end of the Summer Term. This is owing to the large group to be sent to Secondary School after 11 plus.

May 22nd 1963 School closed for school outing to London, Thursday 23rd and Friday 24th May.

> *On the 27th March 1963 the Managers received the news that the school would close when the new infants school had been completed at Yatton. Concerns were expressed by the irregular hours kept by the school in the cold weather. Mrs Griffiths was called in and explained that most of the time Kingston school remained open while other schools were closed for the entire length of the cold spell. Also she was entirely reliant upon the bus for transport and it was not her wish that school should make such a late start. 3 children were to be given Grammar School interviews on the results of the 11-Plus examination.*

June 21st 1963 Headmistress attended the official opening of the new Clevedon Secondary Modern school in Swiss Valley at the invitation of the Chief Ed. Officer.

Ken Kingcott attended Kingston School from September 1958 to July 1965:

My first teacher was Miss Purkis. There were 2 classes of children to cover the ages 4 ½ years up to 11 - these were called the "Babies" and the "Big Ones".
The general regime was very strict under Mrs Griffiths. Certainly some of the children were terrified of her. There was no chatter allowed in the classes and generally it was best to keep your head down and get on with what had to be done. We had to be in school for 9.20am and left at 3.30pm. These times were dictated by the bus time-table as both Mrs Griffiths and, later, Mrs Davies had to travel home by bus.

Assembly was held under the windows in the big room when we sang a hymn and said a prayer. At 11.30 there was a break during which milk had to be consumed; it was very difficult to refuse this and involved letters from parents if you wanted to.

At 12.30 it was lunchtime; the food was cooked at central kitchens in Yatton and delivered in insulated containers which were supposed to keep the food warm; I remember one of the more appetising desserts was treacle tart known as 'sand and gravel'. It was possible, but generally disapproved of, to bring sandwiches into school. Mrs Mary Neath was dinner supervisor for many years and then Mrs Painter, who cycled down from Yatton; they ladled and doled the food out from the containers onto your plate.

Children under eight were picked up by a school car driven by Eddie Baker, it went around the village clockwise. There was great excitement when his car was changed for an old black London taxi cab. After 8 years old, I cycled to school.

Being a Church of England Voluntary Controlled School the catechism had to be learned; about 20 minutes a week were devoted to this. I never did manage to learn it. On Ascension Day (40 days after Easter) we went into church for a talk from the Rev. Rowlands. Then we had the day off.

We had BBC Schools Radio broadcast for P.E (music and movement), singing together, and for science teaching for which there was an accompanying booklet. This was how one learned about weather forecasting and cloud recognition, marine rescue, wildlife observations, etc.

The room was heated by the large cast iron coke stoves which were filled through a plate in the top; there were two in the big room and they were stoked by two of the older boys. I remember the flames shooting out of the top if they hadn't been left to burn down enough when the top was removed.

One positive thing about Mrs Griffiths was that she arranged school outings. In 1960 we went by train from Yatton to Windsor Castle. This was in the days of steam trains, so it was a lot more atmospheric a journey than now, and the train steamed right into Windsor and Eton station which is a dead-end down a 1½ mile branch line.

In 1961 we went to Totnes by train and then walked to the quay, alongside overgrown railway tracks, to a waiting paddle steamer for a trip down the River Dart to Kingswear. Here the train picked us up and took us to Paignton for ¾ of an hour on the beach, while it waited for us in the station, before the return trip to Yatton.

On the River Dart

In 1962 we went to Oxford and to Blenheim Palace. The thing that most impressed me at Blenheim was in a glass case. This was an icing sugar model of the palace. There was also a boat trip on the Thames in a large river-bus where you could break off willow twigs as they brushed past the boat.

Blenheim Palace

197

In 1963 we had the last 'big' outing, this was to London. In this case the engine was a Hawkesworth County Class, which picked us up at Yatton at 7.45 and took us to Paddington. We saw all the famous places by bus - the Houses of Parliament, Fleet Street, Nelson's Column and Pudding Pie Lane where the Fire of London started. Then we went round Westminster Abbey and the Science Museum.

Several children reached 11 the same year and left school in 1963. The following year we went by bus to Clevedon's Salthouse Fields, Holland's Pottery, and Clevedon Court. In 1965 we were taken to Bristol where we went round the Cathedral and Woolworths followed by the Museum.

I left the school in 1965 and did not take much notice of the school afterwards. It was empty in the mornings when we went to catch the coach and in the evenings when we returned.

July 18th 1963 Children performed school plays to an appreciative audience in the Village Hall at a Summer Social Afternoon. The Parents and School Managers were pleased when the Rector assured them that the school would be happily working for a good many years.

July 26th 1963 School closed for the Summer Vacation. Today we had a Leavers' Cricket Match and Picnic. The children presented the Headmistress with gifts. The children were given books by the Headmistress.

Sept 2nd 1963 School re-opened. Number on books 21. School Wood delivered – 8 baskets.

Sept 9th 1963 Headmistress and School Managers attended a special meeting concerning the proposed new Comprehensive Schools to be built at Portishead, Nailsea, Backwell and lastly Clevedon.

Oct 28th 1963 Mrs Davies leaves today to take up a teaching post at Nailsea Four Oaks Infants School on 1st Nov. The Staff being reduced owing to reduction on Roll to 17.

Nov 4th 1963 School re-opened, now a One Teacher School.

Nov 14th 1963 Mrs Florence Paynter started today as a dinner supervisor.

Miss Hawkins's Class May 1960
Back Row Peter Rogers Roger Bush Peter Stuckey Paul Rogers Graham Parsons
Valerie Parsons Marion Kingcott Susan Travis Ken Kingcott Michael Francis
Front Row Clive Teague Jeffrey Naish (Mary Baber)

1964

Feb 14th 1964   Inspected the low levels of school coke left in school shed, I fell and injured my knees and hands and had severe bruising and shock. Mrs Paynter, school canteen helper, attended to me and I remained at school until 3.30 to dismiss the children.

> *Extract from Managers Minutes 16th April 1964: Mrs Travis sent in her resignation as now her daughter had left the school... and Mrs Esme Chard to be asked to fill the vacancy.*

Sept 23rd 1964   I leave school today to go into hospital.

Sept 24th 1964   VA Thompson, County Staff Headmistress took charge of this school today.

Sept 29th 1964   Mr Waterfall, County Architects Dept, called at the school this morning to inspect sanitation, also general repairs needed.

Oct 1st 1964   A representative from Weston's Biscuit firm called at the school to enquire about the sale of biscuits. I explained that the permanent Headmistress was absent through illness and that I personally do not believe in the sale of such goods in school from a health and dental point of view.

Oct 16th 1964   School re-opened today after yesterday's closure for General Election. Results so far received show a swing towards a Labour Government.

Nov 30th 1964   Another stove installed in the big classroom. Not a new one but one in place of the burnt out stove. At least it is warmer now! Weather has become very much colder after the mild spell during most of Nov.

1965

Jan 12th 1965   Simplex Intelligence Test taken with Gp 4 at 10am this morning.

Some of my memories of Kingston School
by Stewart Bruce

I must have been about 7 or 8 at the time, I'm not sure, but I do remember Mrs Griffiths, the Headmistress. She had just been reading the class a story. When she finished, she set about hearing us all read one by one.
I waited for my turn. I left my desk and went up and stood beside her at her desk. She opened the book in front of her, I started to read. She was Welsh and wore spectacles. She would look over the top of them at you, sometimes you did not know if she was looking at you or not.

I did not like her and she had no time for me. It must have been after dinner because her breath smelt of coffee. I dreaded this as I could not read very well and she knew it. I was subjected to humiliating jibes. I would sometimes, as I did on this occasion, receive a poke in the head with her pen – this hurt! I was not the only one to receive this poke of encouragement.

As I finished, I asked her if I could please go to the toilet. This fell on deaf ears and I was told to go and sit down. I asked her again. She just looked at me over the top of her glasses and this time said nothing. The look was enough. I ended up peeing myself, I was so upset. When the bell rang for home-time, I ran out as fast as I could, and when I got home I cried to my mum. To this day I have never forgotten it.

As time went on, we were given jobs. One such job was that of coal monitor. This was done by two boys, you had to go outside in all winds and weathers and get coal in from the coal shed, bring it in and make up the three fires, two in the big hall and one in the small room. It was hot and dirty work. I only did this job sometimes. Looking back, it was like being in Victorian times.

There were some good things that went on. One winter we had a heavy fall of snow. When we finished school we would get a taxi home but on this occasion Ken and Marion Kingcott had come up to the school with a sledge from the farm to collect us. Peter, Jane and myself got on, Ken and Marion pulled the three of us the mile home. We went past about seven farms, all were milking, you could hear the machines and see the lights on. In the distance it was very dark. This was great fun and some things I shall never forget.

Jan 26th 1965   Allocation Examination held in school today, 5 pupils from this school and 1 from outside. Other children not attending today owing to the fact that this is a one teacher school.

Jan 28th 1965   One stove not working making working conditions unpleasant. Temp of big room 44 degrees F (snow shower outside!).

Jan 29th 1965   Stove repaired – improvement in heating.

Feb 9th 1965   Library van called and exchanged Library Books 120. I have retained project books as they are in use.

Feb 12th 1965   I resigned duties as County Staff Head today after a very pleasant stay. Mrs Griffiths resumes duty.

> *1st August 1965: A notice was received by the Managers that the new Yatton Junior School when built would accommodate Kingston children from the age of 7 to 11.*
> *The Manaagers decided to protest as it would not leave the village school viable, the Yatton Infants School was already overcrowded and ' it was feared that the whole pattern of village life would be spoilt for the children if they were hardly in the village except to sleep.'*

1966

Jan 10th 1966 Radio engineer called at school and assembled the school Television Set. All correct and in order.

Jan 11th 1966 Coke supply used up. Notified Taunton of non-delivery. Unless coke is delivered early tomorrow, I shall have to close school. Attendance low owing to snowy weather. 13 out of 19 present.

Jan 12th 1966 Borrowed a little coke from the Church to start fires.

> *On the 28th January a meeting was held of the Managers with representatives of the Education Authorities to discuss the future of the school. Present were: Preb. Rowlands (Chairman), B Harris, H Simmons, E Norton, Mrs Chard. Mrs Kingcott, Mrs Griffiths, Mr Bryce (Educ Officer), Mr Moorland (Chairman of the Somerset Educ Committee), County Councillors Starks and C Stuckey and Preb Franklyne (Diocesan Representative).*

Mr Bryce gave the benefits of having larger primary schools, Mr Moorland said it was proposed that when the new Junior School in Yatton was built the present Junior School would be turned into a Infants School by September 1967. Mr Simmons felt that the proposal would 'strike at the root of village life'. *Mrs Kingcott was unhappy about the time it would take to bus the children to and from the village. Mr Harris said the School was in very good repair and could hold 50 children or more. Mrs Griffiths said there were benefits in the individual attention she could give to smaller groups of children.*

At the parent's meeting which immediately followed 19 were present. Mr Burdge a manager of Yatton Infants School was not at all happy at the prospect of more children because of overcrowding. Other parents stated they were happy with the current system and unanimously voted to keep the school open.

Feb 23rd 1966 4 children away. Influenza still in the village.

Report on Religious Instruction held 16th Feb 1966:

It must be unique for an old scholar, after 50 years, to return to inspect his old school, doomed it seems to closure. But it was so good to find the Church Faith still being taught here as completely and as devoutly as in my boyhood. The opening worship was a reality and the short silence at the school, most impressive. Mrs Griffith's careful work covering the whole syllabus in two little classes, is evident by the childrens' correct and eager replies. Bible, Prayer Book, New Catechism, are all used with the variety of expression work, and last but most important the children know their Church of All Saints and use it.

Wilfred S Griffin (Rev)

May 3rd 1966 Miss Kellet H.M.I. visited the school to inspect all schoolwork. She was very pleased. She remarked on the free, happy, friendly atmosphere.

June 30th 1966 School closed for half day for the Headmistress to take the children to visit Bristol Cathedral and Museum.

15th July 1966 Two men visited school to measure classrooms for re-wiring the electric light. 8 lights are to be installed in the main room instead of the present two, a light in the school kitchen and one outside light at the school entrance door.

July 22nd 1966 6 children leave today.

Extract from Managers Minutes 21ˢᵗ August 1966: The vicar Rev A T Wright, now Curate in Charge of the Parish, was elected as Chairman. Mrs Griffiths intended retiring at the end of the summer term. 14 Children at the school, one of which would be taking the 11-Plus in January. It was unanimously agreed to fight to retain the school if any notification of closure was issued.

Sept 5ᵗʰ 1966 School re-opens. No. on books 14. One entrant.

Sept 10ᵗʰ 1966 Mr Dennis H.M.I. visited school and suggested that the small classroom be used during the winter and the large classroom free for 'play' etc and dining, this he thought would be warmer for winter.

Oct 10ᵗʰ 1966 Area County Surveyor called at school to examine faulty heating stove in large classroom. He decided it could not be repaired and has ordered a new stove to be installed. At present the room is only partially heated.

Nov 19ᵗʰ 1966 New stove installed in large classroom, all is satisfactory.

Jane Bell (Kingcott) was at the school when it finally closed. Most of the following is summarised from her booklet *Some Memoirs of the Last Years of Kingston Seymour School* (2008)

Caroline Chard and Mike Wallis used to go home for lunch so some of us gave them pocket money to buy us sweets from Mrs Summerell's shop. When Mrs Griffiths found out what was going on she put a stop to it abruptly. She strongly disapproved of us entrusting someone else with our money.
I can recall one day when the more compassionate side of this severe teacher broke through her thick veneer. In October 1966 came the devastating reports of the Aberfan disaster, which shocked the whole nation and much of the world. The news came through on television while we were waiting to watch a schools programme. The next day as we were gathered around the piano at morning prayers, Mrs Griffiths was hardly able to keep her composure, crying and unable to complete the prayer. She broke down but just managed to say, "I went to that school..." We had to abandon the rest of the morning prayers and allow her to weep for a few minutes while we listened silently. The majority of the children killed were of

junior school age-group; many of them between the ages of seven and ten years old. Being the same age as so many of the children that were killed, this tragedy in another Victorian-built school, not so many miles away from Kingston Seymour, sticks in my memory.

On the 23rd December 1966 The Managers received a letter from the Education Sub Committee wherein it was stated that they were recommending the closure of the school when the Headmistress retired. The only concession granted was that of allowing the school to remain open until the retirement of the Headmistress instead of when the new Yatton School opened.

1967

Extract from Managers' Minutes 10th April 1967: Mrs Griffiths' letter of resignation was read, it was stated that a decision of the School's future would be taken in June and if she felt she could postpone her retirement until Xmas it would be much appreciated. This she agreed to do. 15th August 1967. The notice of Closure of the school served by the Education Committee of the Somerset County Council. Mr H Simmons proposed and Mrs E Chard seconded a motion that a letter of appeal be made to the Under Secretary of State to allow the school to remain open. This was unanimously agreed and it was decided to procure as many parent's signatures as possible.

Sept 4th 1967 School re-opened. No. on books 12.
Note: this is the first entry for 1967.

Sept 21st 1967 Miss Kellett H.M.I. visited school and discussed the closure of the school with the Headmistress. No date of closure has yet been given.

Nov 17th 1967 P.C. Ship and P.C. Brown visited and showed the children films and gave a Road Safety Talk.

Dec 15th 1967 Mr Bryce from the County Office called and told the Headmistress that the Ministry had given permission to close the school. The date would probably be February Half Term. The Headmistress notified the parents and the School Managers who were present at the Christmas School Nativity Play that afternoon. They agreed that Feb 1968 was the earliest date for closure.

1968

Feb 5th 1968 Miss Saville, Headmistress of Yatton Infants School, called today to discuss and choose stationery and books and equipment she needed for Yatton Infants School.

> *Extract from Managers Minutes 5th Feb 1968; Matters arising that the Secretary of State had sided with the Education Authorities in the matter of the school closure... Mrs Griffiths gave a report of how she was coping with the disposal of school property not required by Yatton Schools. Surplus desks were offered to children at a nominal fee of 5/- per desk and 2/6 per chair as school souvenirs. The Chairman then thanked Mrs Griffiths for her faithful service and hard work she had given the school during her 16 years of office and for the high standard of teaching maintained throughout. He then warmly thanked Mrs Kingcott for all the time she had freely given to the school's affairs during her period as correspondent.*

Feb 6th 1968 Mr Burgess, Headmaster of Yatton Junior School, visited and chose the books and equipment he needed for Yatton Junior School. He also discussed the children's grouping and transfer cards with the Headmistress. The School Piano and Television set is to be sent to Yatton Infants.

Feb 12th 1968 Mr Baker, Welfare Officer called today and discussed transport arrangements of the children to Yatton Schools as from Wed 21st Feb 1968.

Feb 16th 1968 Parents, managers, pupils past and present visited the school today and made a presentation to the Headmistress who is retiring after 41 and half years teaching service. They also wished her a happy retirement. School closed today and the children move to Yatton Infant and Junior Schools on Wednesday 21st.

I terminate my duties today as Headmistress of Kingston Seymour V.C. School after 15 and half years. I have been very happy at this Village School and retire to-day after 41 and half years teaching service. I wish the children a happy future at their new schools at Yatton. The school has been open for 114 years.

Olive Griffiths – Headteacher 16.2.68

The Final Managers' Report

On February 16th 1968 at 2.30pm a large collection of parents, friends and old pupils met in the large schoolroom and after a short speech by Mr A E Harris in which he publicly thanked the Headmistress and expressed his regret at the enforced closure of the school which was another blow to our village life, Mrs Griffiths was presented with a 400 day clock as a mark of esteem from grateful parents and past pupils whom she has got to know so well during the past 16 years.

The present pupils then presented her with a pot plant procured from their own money. In her return speech of thanks, Mrs Griffiths said that we must all remember that school was not just a building of wood and stone but a way of life implanted in each child, all the pupils having passed through the village school would always retain some part of it wherever they went.

The dinner supervisor Mrs Paynter and the Caretaker Mrs Neath were also presented with pot plants, as a farewell gift from the managers, and the correspondent presented with a lovely bunch of tulips.

After cups of tea all round the School was finally left bare and silent.

16th February 1968 The Last Day
Back Row Jane Kingcott Phillip Simmons Caroline Chard Peter Kingcott Mrs Griffiths Stuard Bruce
Front Row Deborah Bailey Stephanie Cox Jeremy Summerell Suzanne Chappell Sandra Chard Nigel Chappell

Official opening of the North Somerset Drainage Board offices in Kingston Seymore school 26th May 1971

Back Row SG Dyer R Cox (viewer) HM Stowell A Frank R Grey AE Brown (Clerk)
J Triggol P Hoy (SRA) LS Grey FA Kingcott LG Edwards (WMIDB) EP Harris
WL Brake AH Tarr JA Franklin A Sweet
Front Row A Huxtable AJ Parker EL Kelting (SRA) MH Crossman (Chaiman)
C Cook (WMIDB) WG McEwen Smith

Chapter 14
What Came After

Gill Harris writes about the North Somerset Drainage Board
Offices in The Old School, Kingston Seymour, from 1969 to 1981:

Mr A.E.W. Brown was Clerk to the North Somerset Internal
Drainage Board from 1960 to 1985. He and his mother lived at
School House. Ted was an accountant, played the church organ and
was the Drainage Board Clerk on a part-time basis. When the
Local Authority sold the adjacent school in 1969 it seemed too
good an opportunity for the drainage board to turn down at £1,750.
In doing so, it took over all the fixtures and fittings, such as they
were.

As the work increased, I joined the board as his assistant in 1976.
The front classroom was used as an office and the infants' room for
Board meetings, maps, etc. No structural changes were made to the
building or to the old playground and toilet block.

Of the furniture, the ship's bell mounted on the south-west outside
wall was donated to the new village hall in 1976. Ken Kingcott
bought one of the teacher's desks and my husband the other. The
children's desks went into the church stables to be stored and more
recently have been sold to various individuals around the village.

Ted Brown sold School House and moved to Tickenham. The
school itself was sold to Rene Kingcott in 1981 and the Board's
office was also transferred to Tickenham, returning to Kingston
Seymour (Mendip View Farm) when I took over as Clerk in 1985.

The Weavers 1977-2003

By Marion Pudner (nee Kingcott)

My mother Rene Kingcott had been interested in spinning and weaving since she bought an old loom with some wool from Clevedon Sale Rooms in the late 1960s. She later learnt to spin and weave from an old lady who lived at Portishead called Miss Norah Sinnock. She was so captivated by it that she attended Frome College and took an A-level in weaving. She also joined the Somerset Guild of Weavers, Dyers and Spinners, which resulted in requests for her to teach. This she started doing in the large attic of Ham Farm. In 1977 my mother was given permission to use the empty room at the school to put on a craft exhibition as part of the village festivities. Having cleaned up the room for the show, she then asked if she could lease it on a permanent basis thus relieving

The small room in later use as a gathering for the Mothers Union. The old Poor Map is hung on the wall. Several old pupils are in this picture.

the overcrowding in her house. Her family had by this time were becoming used to seeing strange ladies wandering around the house!

After approaching various bodies for advice, she then started further education classes funded by the local authority which enabled the school to pay its way. In 1981 the school building was put up for auction and Rene bought it. Over the years she had many pupils from as far away as Portishead, Winscombe and Weston. The big attraction of the centre was that the weavers could leave their work undisturbed on the looms from one session to the next. She collected a variety of looms over the years, some large freestanding ones and other smaller table looms.

When Rene reached retirement age the local authority withdrew funding but the weavers continued with classes all day on Wednesdays and also Thursday evenings. The big room housed most of the bigger looms while the smaller room had spinning wheels and some smaller table looms. There was a big table left from the drainage board days and this came in very useful.

Other meetings also took place there including the Mothers' Union and the Sunday School which Rene ran with Sue Thomas and Joan Ridley.

The large Poor Rate Overseers Map of Kingstone Seamoor (sic), which had been hung in John Hodge and Co. offices in Yatton was eventually given to Ken Stuckey as chairman of the Kingston Seymour Local History Society. It was hung on the wall of the small classroom as being the best place in the village for it at the time. Eventually this map was given over to the custody of the Local Records Office at Taunton and a copy was made for display in the church.

After Rene died in 2001, the spinners and weavers continued at the school but eventually my sister and I sold the building in August 2003. On June 14th 2003 we held an open day there and many old pupils and villagers came. The weavers put on an exhibition of their work, while the History Society and the Drainage Board all displayed photographs. Cream teas were served in the yard and the sun shone all day.

What a lovely way to remember the old building which held so many memories for so many people...

School reunion Saturday 27th June 1998
The cake was cut by Elsie Sampson who was previously Miss Buxton.

A painting of the large room by Patrick Collins
when it was a weaving school

The school today by David Skelton the present owner.

Since buying the School in 2005, we have turned a rather sad and neglected building into a beautiful family home. The black beams have been cleaned to reveal the lovely honey coloured wood underneath. A mezzanine floor has been added, so you can see out of the dormer windows! The main hall is now an open-plan kitchen, dining and living area, flooded with light from the huge window. The main entrance has been tiled in traditional Victorian geometric tiles in terracotta, cream and black. We have tried to carry out the renovation sympathetically while including up-to-date under-floor heating and insulation.

Although the building has been transformed, we think it is still recognisable as the old school. Past pupils who have seen it were impressed, anyway!

A Final Word from Gus Fletcher

When I last visited the old school in June 2003, it was thronged with elderly people, who, like me, were amazed to be meeting together after well over 60 years. Such is the power of the place that some had travelled from afar to get there and it was a happy occasion, albeit tinged with sadness. I passed by again, later in the same year, and the school, now bereft of the June throng of nostalgic old boys and girls, was silent and shuttered, dreaming no doubt, of former days and of many hundreds of children it had educated, nurtured and helped to shape as future citizens of this country. Of course, it is the teachers who make the school, not the stones and the mortar. But in those stones, I feel, there must be instilled some spirit, some sort of zeitgeist as a result of those hundreds of little ones sitting there over the past 100-odd years. Perhaps the people who will live there in the years to come may feel a little of this, and they might even hear, if they listen carefully, very faintly from what was once our playground, and is now, no doubt, or will be one day, their garden, a faint echo of 'Oranges and Lemons' or 'In and out of the Windows'. And perhaps, also, when the house falls silent, late at night and the TV set is switched off, the occupants may hear the faint squeak of chair legs on wooden floors, and, even more faintly, the scrape of chalk on the blackboard. They need have no fear of ghosts however: if there are any in and around the dear old school, and well there may be, they will be, every one of them, friendly spirits.

Headteachers

☐
☐-☐
Mr James Flack
Confirmed in ☐ census wife ☐
and children ☐ ☐

☐-☐
Mr A Turner

☐-☐
Mrs Blanche Jackson

☐-☐
Mr James Smith

April ☐
Mr Smith died ☐

May ☐
Mr Arthur Temporary ☐

☐-☐
Mr William J Sheppard

☐
Mrs and Miss Smith left ☐

☐-☐
Mrs Amy Sheppard Temporary as
husband at war ☐

☐-☐
Mr Wm J Sheppard ☐

☐-☐
Miss Hole

☐-☐
Mrs Brown ☐

☐-☐
Mrs Maslen

☐-☐
Mrs Muriel Coghill ☐

☐-☐
Miss E G Bate ☐
☐
☐-☐
Mrs Olive Griffiths

Rectors

☐
☐-☐
Rev George Octavius Smyth
Pigott

January ☐ Rev G O Smyth
Pigott died

Rev G H Smyth Pigott son of
the above ☐

☐-☐
Rev M R R Green

☐ Rev Green died ☐

☐-☐
Rev Harold Arthur Cottrell

☐-☐
Rev Frank Howard Gornall

☐-☐
Rev Percy William Reece
Rowlands

☐
Rev Trevor Wright

☐-☐
Rev Frank Stevens

Headteachers	Rectors
Headteachers	**Rectors**
1860 – 1872 Mr James Flack Confirmed in 1861 census wife and children 7 & 3.	1854 – 1892 Rev. George Octavius Smyth-Pigott
1872 – 1875 Mr A Turner	
1875 – 1882 Mrs Blanche Jackson	January 1892 Rev G.O. Smyth-Pigott died
1882 – 1912 Mr James Smith	Rev. G.H. Smyth-Pigott (son of the above)
April 1912 Mr Smith died.	1905 – 1935 Rev. M. R. R. Green
May 1912 Mr Arthur (Temporary)	
1912 – 1916 Mr William J Sheppard	
1913 Mrs and Miss Smith left	
1916 – 1919 Mrs Amy Sheppard (Temporary as husband at war)	
1919 – 1922 Mr Wm J Sheppard	
1922 – 1927 Miss Hole	1935 Rev. Green died
1927 – 1930 Mrs Brown	1935 – 1938 Rev. Harold Arthur Cottrell
1930 – 1937 Mrs Maslen	1938 – 1946 Rev. Frank Howard Gornall
1937 – 1943 Mrs Muriel Coghill	1946 – 1966 Rev. Percy William Reece Rowlands
1943 – 1952 Miss E. G. Bate	1967 Rev. Trevor Wright
1953 – 1968 Mrs Olive Griffiths	1968 – 1974 Rev. Frank Stevens

Name index .

Cane 89
Carpenter, 100,101,103,134, Albert 110, Bernard 169, Cynthia 163,
Frank 107,113, Gladys 132,134,136, Grantley 118, Gwen 139,140,141,
Joyce 139, Maurice 163, Winnie 116,
Carver 113,114,119,133
Case 120
Chappell 157,163,164,168,169,170,181,183,207
Chard 200,202,204,205,207
Clark 67,71,77,78,82-84,,87,148
Clarke 68,87,101,107
Claxton PC 157,161
Claydon 161-164
Clements 38
Cleverdon 57,62,67,72,75,76
Colbourne or Cobern Alice 41, Tommy 28, 29,31, Frances 29,
Sidney 29,
Cole 181
Coles 70,96
Collins 212
Cook 43,45
Cooke 44,50 Dr. 109,188
Coombes 29
Coombs 22,27,29,31
Corfield 49
Cottrell 126
Cox Barbara 89,92, Beatrice 61,77, Edith 42, Elsie 43,52,71, F 93,
George 30,39, Harry 30,43, Jim 114, Joseph 46,71, Sam 114,
Stephanie 207, Susannah 77, V 93, William 53,64,65
Crook 68
Crossman 208

Davey 41,42
Davies 38-65, Elsie 99, Miss 111-117 Mrs 192-198
Davis 41
Dean 62
De Molegns 12,15
Denmead A 19, Rachel 7, H 19, J 27
Dixon 51
Draper 155,156
Durbin John 7,Dorothy 123

Earl John 7
Edwards 36,38,39
Eddington Thomas 7
Eglington/Eglinton 30,41,43,61,64,87,107,113,144
Elliot EHB 34,51
Elton 85
Evans 96,107

Fisher AB 67, Theodore 14
Fitzgerald 124
Fry 16,50
Flack James 9
Fletcher F 134,145, Gus134,139, 143,213, R 132,134,136,145,
T 29,68,69, Wm 26
Flower 30,55,65
Friar 105
Forbes 106
Ford Agnes 68,73,87, Arthur Vivian 73,74,87,92, Bob
54,126,134,139,152, Cecil 59,62,77,85, Doris 55,61, Edwin 55,
Harold 55, John 73, Kate 92,98, Marigold 132,134,137,141, T 84
Foster and Wood 9
Fountain 134,153-161
Fowler 30
Francis 199
Franklin or Franklyne 180,202
Fuller Dr. 48,63,65,83

Gabriel 47
Gage 9,26, 37
Gardener, Gardiner, Gardner 29,30,41
Gatehouse 73
Glastenbury 77,83,114
Glassenbury, 42,96,101,106,107,115,118,119
Godfry 44
Godfrey 57,67
Gooding E 18, Henry 11, Harriet 13
Goodliffe 57,68,71,84
Gornall 138-157
Gould 8,9,25
Grant 174
Gratham 43
Green Rev.60-126
Gregory 41
Grevile E C 7
Grant 159
Grey 91
Griffin 48,54,164,173, Alfred 27-77, Bernard 66,87,90,92,93, Betty 104,
Bird 87, Brian 161,162,164,181, Charles 25, Donald 106, Dorothy
132,134,136, 141, Edna 134,140,141 Edgar 107, Edward 49, Elizabeth
108,Ernest 185, Frank 73,87,114, Fred 44, Graham 163,169, Hartley 44,
Janet 183, Lesley 47,79, Mary 103,108,109,185, May 41, Megan
104,113,114,122, Mervyn 96,110,113, Monica 163,181, Pat 183, Reg 87,
185, Roland 20,185, S 22,Samuel Austen 79, Stanley 41, Sydney 81, Vera
134,141, Winnie 43,47, Wilfred 81,87,93,119,203

Jowles 57

Kellow 173,176
Kemp,125
Kent 117,118
Kerton 98
Kilminster 171
King John 9,W 70
Kingcott Albert 41,Arthur 41,B 83,92, David 148,157, Edith 119, Frank
129,208, Howard 41, Ivor 137,139, 141,157, Jane 201,204,207 Ken
195,199,201,209 Louise 46,149, Marion 193,199,210, Miss 96-120, Peter
201,207,Rene 178, 191,202,209, 210, William 41
Knapp 116

Lamb 123
Lampert Biddie 113,114,122, Don 113,114, Frank 50, Harry 65, Henry
43, John 44, L. 83, Lilly 56, Mabel 45, Olive 63,73, Percy 57, Philip 182,
Ronald 96,97,111, Sydney 105,113, Wilfred 58, 63,65,73,82,,87
Langford 43
Larder 84,
Latham 96,97
Lauder 99
Lee 85
Lewis 41,93,Edith 119,120
Long 81, 90, Col. 54,62
Loveridge 49
Luff 49,78,82,87,96,114
Lye 66

Marshall Dorothy 117,Rev. 80
Maslen 80,123-132
Masters 84,98,105,106
Mather 57,58
McCleod Dr.
McDougall 97,103,104
Meaker 38,40
Meek 176-190
Melsome Dr. 106
Mills 82,83,87
Miles W 8
Moody 168
Moore 123,
Moorland 202
Morris 41
Mostyn Pryce 63
Munckton 125
Murray 104-107

Naish 45,199
Nash Emily 12
Neads Agnes 9, Pauline 162
Neath, 48,52,62, Ada 58, Alice 41, Alfred 41,57,61, Annie 62, Cecil 113, Edith 26, Edward 45,64, Ernest 58, Frank 30,52, George 30, Harry 29, Jane 28, Jenny 29, Kathleen 183, Lesley 114, Leslie 107,113, Letitia 62, Mary 190,194,207, Olive 43, 62,113,114,119, Rosie 183, Ted 114,119, Walt 113,122,188, Wm 105,113,114
Needham 66
Newman 104,107
Newsome 130
Norris Ernest 57, Harry 59, Robert 24
Norton 160, Alice 68,69,70,87, Bruce 163,169,181, Cecil 148,157, Ernest 75,87,202,Ruth 98,102, Vera 134,139,142, Winifred 113,114

Orchard 105
Orr 142,162,167,177,190
Owen 80

Painter/Paynter 169,196,198,207
Palmer 11,117,153,154,160,161,173, Cassie 111,113, Catherine 107, Denzil 113,114,134, Jack 92,98,113, John 103
Panes 92,93
Parker Dr.75,86,91
Parker 49,50
Paroley 40
Parsley 27, Annie 61,73,77,83, Lilly 29,35
Parsons, A 82, Albert 43, Alfred 90, Arthur 57,84, Barbara 163,169,171 Bert 132,136, Cecil 114, Cyril 105,113, Edith 87, Edward 72,74,76,87, Edwin 105,113,114, Elsie 66, Enid 129,134, Gillian 61,Graham 181,194,199,Harold 148, Howard 183, Julie 41, L 96, Michael 163,181, Olive 98,107, Valerie 194,199
Payne Joseph 32,36
Pearce 57,70,142,157
Phippen 41,71
Pigott B 15
Piggott 16, C 22
Pine 170
Pitts 51,53,55
Plumbley 67,74
Plumley 62,72
Pope 96
Pople 93
Powell 87,91,93,96 , Doug 113, James 107,111, Jim 113,114, Judith 163, Margaret 98,103,104,Oliver 163
Price 54,107,111,114,125

Studley 41,42
Summerell 132-137,139,141,148,162,168,207
Summers 30,37,41,59,76
Sweet A 208, Alan 63,66,76, Dick 87, Elsie 74,87 F 66, H 97, Hilda
75,83, Joyce 90,93,98, Phyllis 92,93,98, Richard 67,68

Taylor 70,71
Teague 199
Tipper 27,35,37,38
Tilly 29
Thomas 42 Sue 211
Thompson 200-201
Tombs 56
Tones 84
Towell 51
Towser 114
Towzer 67
Tozer 109,116
Travis Frank 105, Gladys 178,191, Grace 102, Jack 98,102,103,113,125,
Joan 163,171,181, John 163, Sue 192,194,199, William 49,77, 129,170
Traves 29,67,90,98,102
Trott 93
Tuck 107
Tucker 30,49,57
Turner 10,15,17,18,80
Tutton 47,48

Uden 42
Usher 142

Vawdrey 119,138,161,162,164
Vaughan 50,57,58,75
Veale 183
Vowells 107
Vowles 87,96

Wallis 164,168,169, Anne 163 ,165,169, Cyril 98,113, Dennis 96,98,103,
113,114,125,131, Edgar 76,140, 175, Edith 62, George 44,46, Hannah 14,
James 7, John 9,54,55,62,173, 175,183, Joyce 129, Louise 46,47,
Kathleen 194, Mike 204, Roy,132,136,161, Willie 44,46, Samuel 9
Watts 68,70
Wayford 42
Waygood 29,38,58
Weaver Dr. 108

Webber 72,134, Blanche 39, Daisy 30,57, Dorothy 44, Flo 29,30, Kath 67,71,78,83, Kay 102,125, Lilly 29,31, Mabel 30, May 87, Norah 62,71, Winnie 9,71,78,83,87,125
Westoversoon 7
Willard 41
Williams 15, A 91, B 22, Gillian 163,181, Gratton 113,114,116, Ida 110,111, James 26, Lesley 96, Mervyn 103,106,113,114,119
Wilson 105,181
Windmill 105,107
Witherall 7
Wood Dr. 106,120,,Mrs 106
Woodforde 9
Woodman 41
Wooster 152-153
Wright 204
Wynn 140,141

Yearsley 42
Yelverton 85,86,90,91
Young Alice 61, Beatrice 35,6, Beryl 98, Charles 76,87, Gladys 72,87,90, John 48, Margaret 41,51,52, Polly 66,73,76,79, Sarah 36, Winnie 73